All the B...

Tom Klobuchar

PRAISE FOR
THE GREAT WORKPLACE REVOLUTION

"Tom Klobucher's book is a blueprint for how CEOs should interact with employees across the generations, and keep their customers happy and coming back."

—C. James Carr, CEO
Blue Book Services

"A must-read for CEOs and leaders engaged in hiring and retaining creative knowledge workers for today and the future. A communication roadmap to help you navigate through multiple generations in the workplace."

—Ralph Kuehn, CEO
Building Service, Inc.

"A fascinating book that will forever change the way you look at the workplace."

—Roy Keech, Retired Senior Vice President,
Herman Miller, Inc.

"Inspired and inspiring advice on motivating and keeping a great team."

—Bob Bowers, CEO,
Soliant Consulting, Inc.

"Having worked with multi-generational businesses for 25 years, I know the difficulties that intergenerational dynamics can present. Tom Klobucher's book is an excellent tool for any business needing to deal with these dynamics. He lays it all out in black and white—the issues and the solutions."

—Edwin Hoover, Ph.D.,
Co-author of *Getting Along In Family Business:
The Relationship Intelligence Handbook*

MORE PRAISE FOR
THE GREAT WORKPLACE REVOLUTION

"Extremely insightful and strategic thinking for every workplace owner to optimize and retain the best creative people for maximized results. Tom Klobucher speaks from personal experience with proven ideas."

—BRUCE KOENIGSBERG,
Wheaton College Architect,
Wheaton, Illinois

"Creating a Great Place To Work is an awesome theme. Tom Klobucher's twelve strategies will help businesses run more efficiently, keep customers happy, and help you retain the best people in the work force."

—MICHAEL MCMORRAN, President
Five Star Manufacturing, Inc.

THE
GREAT
WORKPLACE
REVOLUTION

THE
GREAT
WORKPLACE
REVOLUTION

Twelve Essential Strategies
For Creating A Great Place To Work

THOMAS S. KLOBUCHER

The Great Workplace Revolution:
Twelve Essential Strategies For Creating A Great Place To Work

Published by

NEXTIS PRESS
476 Brighton Drive
Bloomingdale, Illinois 60108 USA
www.thegreatworkplacerevolution.com

Cover and Interior Design: AuthorSupport.com
Cover Imagery: Thinkstock/Hemera/Photodisc
Author Photography: Michael Hudson Photography

ISBN: 978-0-9848469-0-0
Mobi ISBN: 978-0-9848469-1-7
ePub ISBN: 978-0-9848469-2-4

Printed in the United States of America

Table of Contents

Table of Contents (continued)

ACKNOWLEDGMENTS

First I want to give thanks to God The Father, who loves us all.

To the memory of my father, John Klobucher, who challenged me to dream big dreams, and also taught me about the joy of good work.

To the memory of my dear mother, Rose Ann Klobucher, who made each one of her five children think that she loved that one the most.

To my wife Carol, who is my soul mate, my partner, my best friend and encourager, and the one person who always makes me want to be a better man.

To my children, Lisa and Paul, their spouses, Mark and Amy and my five grandchildren, Kate, Jenna, Seth, Caden, and Kelsy.

To my oldest sister, Rose K. Kammerling, who challenged and guided me as a young man to do the right thing, was always there for me in times of need, and was a solid rock of strength.

To my three additional siblings, Ray, Barbara and Ed, with whom I am blessed.

To all of the associates at our firm, Thomas Interior Systems, who make it a truly Great Place To Work.

Special thanks to you, the reader, for investing in this book. My hope is that you will achieve great success and much fun as you move along on this exciting journey of creating A Great Place to Work.

My gratitude to each person and organization that allowed us to highlight their best practices in this book.

Special thanks to Shep Hyken, a mentor that encouraged me through the entire writing process.

Thank you to Brandon Toropov, of iWordSmith support, my editor and friend who guided and inspired me to stay the course.

Many thanks to Victoria Wright, of Bookmark Services, who did the final rounds of editing, along with cheering me on across the finish line.

Thank you to Jerry Dorris at AuthorSupport.com for the cover design and layout of the book interior, along with much advice along the way.

To my long time friend, Ed Hoover, who was the first person to tell me that I needed to write this book.

Thanks to Dan Sullivan, Founder of the Strategic Coach, Inc., who inspired me in my entrepreneurial journey, and in this book project.

Grateful thanks to each one who made generous comments of praise about this book.

FOREWORD

Tom often says, "I don't know why I know that, I just do."

"Why are you writing a book?" People have asked my dad, Tom, this question countless times, in a variety of tones, since he decided to begin this book project over a year ago. Dad has always had a good response. But then, "Why?" is a question Tom has faced before. "Why are you starting an office furnishings company?" When Tom started Thomas Interior Systems, Inc. in the late '70s it's safe to say people weren't running to start new office furnishings firms, yet Tom saw a growing need that wasn't being addressed by his peers. The 35 successful years of Thomas Interior Systems are proof of his ability to see a need before most other people do.

I can attest that this is a maddeningly accurate ability of his. As I was growing up, his intuition saved me from buying a Honda CRX hatchback and a scooter (on more than one occasion). And his innate ability has helped our company stay ahead of industry/economic trends in times, both good and bad.

Now it has led him to write this book.

Why does a CEO of a successful office furniture business use his time and energy to accomplish this task? Knowing him as I do, I can tell you that it makes perfect sense. There has been much research done, and many books written, about elements of this topic, but none of these combine the data as he has done. Not one of them offers the sensible, humane, and clear solution to the question that plagues business leaders around the world: "How do I create a great place to work that attracts and retains the best and brightest talent?" Tom saw this gap, and rather than wait for someone else to address it, he just did it.

It's important to note that my dad and I are both "quick starts." The idea of writing a book comes easily to us, as does designing the book's cover, and maybe even writing an outline for the book. What is more difficult for us quick-start types is the tedious work of actually writing that book. I point this out partly because I am proud of him for staying the course long past where I would have packed it in, but more important, so you know what you are about to read. This is not just one more book by someone who writes for a living. This is a lifetime of learning and observing business environments and cultures from around the country, combined with hard data, with one very clear purpose: to improve the office work environment.

All of this work was done through the lens of a successful

entrepreneur with a passion for adding value to everything he does. This led him to start Thomas Interior Systems, to serve on the boards of many organizations, and now to write this book. The answer to the first question in this foreword, why did he write this book, is actually a simple one: He just had to.

This book provides a roadmap for a journey that is neither short nor easy, but one which has an incredible reward at the end: A Great Place to Work. In my opinion, this is one of the most important things you, as a business leader, can spend your time creating. Tom and I both wish you luck, wisdom, and determination as you move along this exciting journey.

Paul Klobucher, President

Thomas Interior Systems, Inc.

INTRODUCTION:
ON THE ART OF TAILORING

"Find joy in work, and discover the fountain of youth."
— **Pearl S. Buck** (1892–1973),
American author, Nobel laureate

"Men do not quit playing because they grow old;
they grow old because they quit playing."
— **Oliver Wendell Holmes, Sr.** (1809–1894),
American physician, professor, and author

"The best job is the one you have now ...
but you can always make it better."
— **John Klobucher**

MAKING IT BETTER

My dad, John Klobucher, came to the United States from Eastern Europe in 1913 at the age of seventeen, made it through all the immigration processing checkpoints at Ellis Island, and then set out, all alone, to make something of himself in his new country. He was an entrepreneur at heart, and after working in a variety of occupations in the East and Midwest, he found his life's calling. In 1922, he opened a custom tailor's shop, Klobucher's Klothes, in La Salle, Illinois. He devoted the next fifty-five years of his life to that business, married my mother, raised five children, and made Klobucher's Klothes a thriving enterprise. By the standards of his time, that business was extremely successful because, in the depths of the Great Depression, people came from as far as a hundred miles away to have their suits made by my father. (Remember, we're talking about a time when making the ninety-mile journey from, say, Chicago to La Salle to be fitted for a suit was a major undertaking.)

We lived behind the storefront. I remember many times when, as a young boy, silent and hidden away behind the clothes racks, I watched my father as he talked with his customers, determining exactly what that person needed and detailing the perfect suit for him, the suit that spoke to the man he wanted to be, the person he wanted to become for himself and his family. These were remarkable discussions to listen to, and they often had more to do with learning about a customer's philosophy of life than with learning about what kinds of fabric and styling the customer preferred.

My father's business succeeded in financial terms because it succeeded on human terms. It succeeded because he was deeply committed to giving his customers a whole lot more than a suit. He was committed to giving them their own best version of themselves. That left an enduring impression on people. And when I say enduring, I mean enduring. Recently, in my research for this book, I spoke with a Chicago-area banking executive who told me that, over a fifty-five year period, four generations of her family had started their professional careers by buying suits from my father's store!

What I was watching when I eavesdropped on my father's discussions with his customers was about tailoring clothes, but it was also about tailoring something else: A person's self-image. To create the right suit for a customer, my father had to measure more than the dimensions of a customer's figure. He had to take the measure of the man. (Yes, my father's customer base was overwhelmingly male.) That meant finding out who they were, who they hoped to become, and what they wanted to project to the outside world. My father had to build all that into a suit that customers were willing to travel long distances for and pay a lot of money for, a suit they could be married in, apply for a job in, and be buried in. His goal was to give them more than they had paid for. And that meant talking to people in depth.

Listening to my father conduct these discussions was the inspiration for what I eventually came to call "tailored solutions" in my own career, which has been focused on the creation of workspace environments. Following my father's example, I realized that I was not really "selling office furniture," any more than he had been selling cloth and buttons. With every program our company put together for a customer, I tried to make it my business to give them more than what they had bought. I made it my goal to help that company become the kind of company it wanted to become, by helping its employees to become the kind of people *they* wanted to become. To follow my dad's line of thinking, I was helping people to take the job they had now and make it better.

Is it a stretch to imagine that a working environment can improve a company's retention rates for key employees? That it can improve the hiring process? That it can make it easier for executives to communicate meaningfully with their employees, perhaps for the first time? That the right workspace can help an organization move from "You're hired, here's your desk, sit down and get to work" to "Welcome to our company—we hired you because we believe you can become one of our very best employees, so please tell us what you need from us to do the work we are asking you to do"?

Is all of that a stretch? My father wouldn't have thought so, and the client base we have been blessed to work for over the last thirty-five years doesn't seem to think so, either.

PROOF OF CONCEPT

"However beautiful the strategy,
you should occasionally look at the results."
— Winston Churchill (1874–1965),
British politician and statesman

This is not, of course, a book about tailoring clothes, but a book about tailoring great workplaces. For decades, our company's mission has been to help others build great places to work. Over three and a half decades, we have successfully completed more than 20,000 office design projects for customers who wanted to improve the office work environment for their employees.

I offer the following information simply to provide "proof of concept" that the ideas I write about here actually do work. How do I know? Because they have worked for us and for thousands of other companies that have hired us!

Twice in the past six years, Thomas Interior Systems has been honored as one of the top 20 Best Places to Work in Illinois. It was quite an honor to be selected the first time; being selected again was what inspired me to begin writing this book.

The Best Places to Work in Illinois is an annual workplace analysis and competition. Managed by Best Companies Group, the program is sponsored by the *Business Ledger*, the Illinois Chamber of Commerce, and the Illinois State Council of the Society for Human Resource Management (ISC-SHRM). The program was designed to identify, recognize, and honor the best places of employment in Illinois, benefiting the state's economy, its workforce, and its businesses. Companies may be either for-profit or not-for-profit and either publicly or privately held. To be considered for participation, they must have a facility and at least 25 employees in the state of Illinois, and must have been in business for at least one year.

Each year, large-sized (250 or more employees) and medium-sized (25 to 249 employees) companies from across the state enter the two-part process to be considered for recognition. The first part of the evaluation process includes a review of each company's workplace policies, practices, philosophy, systems, and demographics. The second part comprises a comprehensive, confidential employee survey. Best Companies Group then assesses the data with assistance from ModernThink, a workplace excellence consulting firm, in order to determine and rank the top 10 large-sized and top 20 medium-sized companies.

How did we make the cut, not once, but twice? I believe there are twelve answers to that question: twelve essential strategies for building a great workplace. I share all twelve in this book.

I wrote this book because I believe that tailoring is a matter of finding out who someone is, and then creating something—whether it is a suit of clothes or a workspace environment—that is an extension of the person's best personality and highest aspirations. I wrote the book to summarize some hard-won lessons from my own career, and also to summarize important insights from some very wise people who also have created great places to work. I wrote this book to honor my father, although he is no longer alive. I wrote this book so that it would be a help to you and your organization as you learn more about the twelve essential strategies for building a great workplace... and about the often-overlooked task of becoming a generational coach in the work environment. And finally, I wrote this book to help implement our long-standing corporate vision and mission: To improve the office work environment.

PART ONE:
EXECUTIVE SUMMARY

THE KEY POINTS IN A
FEW MINUTES OR LESS

A Great Workplace is made up of many characteristics and personalities. Some elements have to do with the physical environment, furnishings, and decor, but most of the high-impact elements center on the more complex dynamics of human interaction. What follows is a summary of some of the most important elements.

RETAINING THE KNOWLEDGE WORKER

Innovative knowledge workers—the ones everyone wants to retain, regardless of what the larger economy is doing—will determine the fates of whole companies... and whole industries. The question is, will you be in a position to do what is necessary to attract and retain them?

The twenty-first-century knowledge worker must make sense of an ever-changing landscape, one that consists of demographic, social, and economic challenges and career/organizational opportunities. Enterprises that build the workplace around the principles of supporting a generationally diverse workforce and putting creative employees first will be the ones that succeed in the marketplace. This book shows you how to fulfill both objectives.

UNDERSTAND THE FIVE WORKPLACE GENERATIONS

Retaining innovative knowledge workers is difficult or impossible for organizations that do not consider the ages and distinctive demographic perspectives of the people who will be making key contributions.

If your company is like most of those we work with, there are no fewer than four workplace generations now operating in your workplace at the same time, each with its own "language." A fifth is now preparing to enter the workforce, making for unprecedented generational diversity in the workplace, starting around the year 2020. The ability of these five groups to interact harmoniously and creatively is a major strategic priority for your enterprise! That means you need someone to translate for, and interact with, all five of demographic groups. I call this person the Great Workplace Revolution Coach.

Beware! Treating these five demographic groups as identical as you plan or upgrade your organization's workspaces is demographic bigotry. That can cost you and your enterprise dearly in terms of employee attraction, retention, productivity, and competitive advantage.

TRADITIONALISTS: Born before 1946, their primary values are DEPENDABILITY and SACRIFICE.

THE BABY BOOMERS: Born between 1946 and 1964, their primary values are CHALLENGING LIMITS and QUESTIONING EVERYTHING.

GENERATION X: Born between 1965 and 1976, their primary value is INDEPENDENCE.

THE MILLENNIALS: Born between 1977 and 1997, their primary values are FUN and CONNECTION.

COMING SOON: GENERATION 2020: Born around the year 2000, they are described as

- Connected.

- Concerned.

- Careful.

- Collaborative.

TWELVE ESSENTIAL STRATEGIES FOR BUILDING A GREAT WORKPLACE

One person, the Great Workplace Revolution Coach, must be able to speak the languages of all five of these generations and must also be able to unite them in a single cause. As the case studies in this book suggest, there are twelve proven strategies for launching and supporting this cause *internally,* so that your organization can deliver great service to its *external* customers. Those twelve strategies are:

1. Great Workplace Revolution Strategy #1: Identify the organization's core values and talk about those values frequently with customers and employees.

2. Great Workplace Revolution Strategy #2: Design and constantly refine a creative workplace based on direct employee feedback.

3. Great Workplace Revolution Strategy #3: Put the right person in the right job.

4. Great Workplace Revolution Strategy #4: Provide constant accommodation to, and understanding of, the whole employee.

5. Great Workplace Revolution Strategy #5: Build into the workplace culture appropriate recognition for a job well done.

6. Great Workplace Revolution Strategy #6. Support a truly collaborative workplace, both physically and emotionally.

7. Great Workplace Revolution Strategy #7: Appoint someone Director of Fun.

8. Great Workplace Revolution Strategy #8: Create after-work events that involve direct personal contact with customers and employees.

9. Great Workplace Revolution Strategy #9: Give something back to the community.

10. Great Workplace Revolution Strategy #10: Ensure that each employee's work space makes good ergonomic sense.

11. Great Workplace Revolution Strategy #11: Invest in ongoing education and personal development.

12. Great Workplace Revolution Strategy #12: Give employees regular feedback.

Now it's time to get to work. Figure out who your Great Workplace Revolution Coach is (maybe it's you!) and give that person the authority to connect with people and change the status quo.

PART TWO:
WHY A REVOLUTION?

THE WORKSPACE REVOLUTION: MEETING THE CHALLENGE OF PRESENTEEISM

Find a job you like, and you add five days to every week.

— H. Jackson Brown, Jr.,
Author of bestselling *Life's Little Instruction Book*

One of the reasons I decided to write this book was to combat a major challenge that most workplaces in America are now facing, a challenge that America itself must overcome if it is to remain a global leader in the twenty-first century: the problem of presenteeism.

You have probably already heard of the problem of absenteeism. That's when workers don't show up at all, either because they have a valid excuse (illness, emergency, or severe weather, for example), or because they simply don't feel like coming in, and don't bother to give management any reasonable explanation for their absence.

The classic business-school response to absenteeism is that employees should be on site, in the facility, and ready to work nineteen out of every twenty calendar days.

This standard is not enough. Now, the main thing I want to point out about this standard—leaving aside the question of whether it is right for any given organization—is that it is quantifiable. That's probably one of the reasons it is so popular as a management benchmark.

The problem of presenteeism is much more difficult to measure.

SPOTTING PRESENTEEISM IN THE WORKPLACE

"The world is full of willing people, some willing to work, the rest willing to let them."

— **ROBERT FROST** (1874–1963), American poet

On any given day, some percentage of your workforce is present, but performing significantly below its true potential. The workers in question have showed up, and are technically present, but they are not "all there."

These employees may have showed up for work sick, or hung over, or profoundly distracted because of some pressing family emergency. They may even have showed up unmotivated because of a sense of disillusionment with the workplace itself, which is the part we as leaders can have the biggest impact on. How? Here is the shortest answer: By making it easy to have fun. If there is no fun in the workplace, you can bet there is no spirit, either! Fun is the antidote to presenteeism.

If you have ever had the experience of knowing or strongly suspecting that an employee was looking for another job while on your payroll, you have had direct experience with presenteeism. Such employees are present in body, but absent in spirit. Because spirit counts, we should be concerned about presenteeism.

Presenteeism is a documented phenomenon of great interest to academics, and there's been quite a bit of research on it in recent years. For the purposes of this book, I am expanding the practical definition of the term somewhat, so that it includes not only factors that are generally beyond the reach of management, but also factors like the lack of a sense of challenge or the absence of a clear personal development path.

Although it's difficult, or perhaps impossible, to measure the level of presenteeism in a specific workplace at any given moment, and although presenteeism is not something we should expect to be able to eliminate entirely, I believe that creating a great place to work is one of the very best ways to counteract this challenge. To put the matter bluntly, some organizations have far fewer restless employees who wish they were somewhere else than other organizations.

These organizations do a better job of tailoring the workspace to individual workers. This customization of the workplace, for both individuals and teams, is based on generational, career-path-driven, and skill set elements that combine to make each team, and each employee who is worth retaining, a unique, but solvable, retention puzzle.

I offer the case studies and best practices that make up the heart of this book not as an academic exercise but primarily as the answer to a question that has troubled me for decades: What do organizations with a truly motivated, truly present workforce do to tailor their workspaces and engage their employees?

TROUBLE IN THE WORKPLACE? MAYBE NOT!

Each generation imagines itself to be more intelligent than the
one that went before it, and wiser than the one that comes after it.
— GEORGE ORWELL (1903–1950),
British author and journalist

According to some, there is big generational trouble brewing in the American workplace.

Yet another generation is preparing to enter the US workforce in or around the year 2020, at the same time that many thousands of Baby Boomers will be *re-entering* the workforce after unsuccessful attempts at retirement that were thwarted by economic pressures. There are experts who warn that generational conflict in the workplace is now threatening to change work life as we know it, as no less than five generations—ranging from twenty-somethings to eighty-somethings—struggle with the task of finding work and working side by side.

Is the sky really falling? I don't think so.

I see not trouble but great opportunity as we progress into this Greatest Workplace Decade of All—"The Synergistic Decade," when five distinct generations learn to understand and synergize the unique and very different capacities of each group, and then leverage this cross-pollination to support unprecedented growth and success. I believe the coming decade has the potential to deliver a new age of discovery, innovation, and collaboration, both in the US and around the world, for organizations whose leaders know how to take full competitive advantage of the unique circumstances they face.

To launch a synergistic revolution in your workplace, a revolution that draws effectively on the varied strengths of today's cross-generational teams, you will need to:

- Tailor individual workplaces to the unique strengths and requirements of the most creative workers.

- Make the workplace a place of communal fun, teamwork, engagement, learning, understanding, achievement, and celebration.

- Instill a sense of personal commitment to your organization's mission by supporting the growth and development of employees over time.

I look at all three of these critical strategic goals as non-negotiable competitive imperatives in the dynamic, multigenerational, globally competitive space in which we all must now compete. The best and quickest ways to achieve these objectives in today's enterprise, in my view, is to implement the Twelve Great Workplace Revolution Strategies, all of which are discussed in depth in Part Two of this book.

IS YOUR WORKPLACE GENERATIONALLY CHALLENGED?

With 85 million Baby Boomers and 50 million Gen Xers, there is already a yawning generation gap among American workers, particularly in their ideas of work-life balance. For Baby Boomers, it's the juggling act between job and family. For Gen X, it means moving in and out of the workforce to accommodate kids and outside interests. Now along come the 76 million members of Generation Y [Millennials]. For these new 20-something workers, the line between work and home doesn't really exist. They just want to spend their time in meaningful and useful ways, no matter where they are.

— **PENELOPE TRUNK**, Time Magazine, July 5, 2007.

Believe it: Five strikingly different generations will be sharing the workplace in the year 2020.

That's an unprecedented state of affairs, and one that is already leading to some major challenges in the workplace. Very often, interoffice conflict and miscommunication has its roots in generational differences. Whether you are in management, part of a team, or even on the outside looking in, you should know whether your organization has internal obstacles that make communicating across the generations more difficult than it has to be.

Take this simple five-point assessment to find out whether your organization would benefit from a program for improving intergenerational communication.

1. You have heard, read, or seen someone in your organization over the age of forty-five express resentment, disappointment, surprise, or even anger about a younger colleague wanting too much too quickly. (For example, "He's only been here three months and he expects a raise/promotion.") **TRUE/FALSE**

2. You have heard, read, or seen someone in your organization under the age of forty-five complain about not receiving recognition or positive reinforcement in the workplace. (For example, "Would it kill her to give me a compliment once in a while?") **TRUE/FALSE**

3. A younger employee has shown up for work in an outfit, or wearing a hairstyle, or sporting some form of bodily adornment, that caused older employees to talk about him or her in an unflattering way. **TRUE/FALSE**

4. A group of senior employees or volunteers were asked to take part in a project overseen by a younger manager, and things didn't go well because the older employees didn't feel they were being shown the proper respect. **TRUE/FALSE**

5. A promising younger employee has accumulated significant experience with your organization in a very short period of time, and then left to work for another company with little or no advance notice. **TRUE/FALSE**

If you have experienced, observed, or heard about even ONE of these workplace issues, the odds are good that you have a generational communication problem in your workplace, but haven't yet taken action to address it. To identify the real problems that give rise to experiences like these, and to begin the process of building a workplace environment where good communication among the generations is a daily reality, read on.

THE FIVE WORKPLACE GENERATIONS: THE ULTIMATE OPPORTUNITY FOR CREATIVITY

"Creativity is a lot like looking at the world through a kaleidoscope. You look at a set of elements, the same ones everyone else sees, but then reassemble those floating bits and pieces into an enticing new possibility. Effective leaders are able to do this by means of interactions that make both individuals and groups more likely to look through the telescope."

— ROSABETH MOSS KANTER,
Harvard Business School professor

The first and most important question to consider as you begin to learn about the five workplace generations is this one: *Are you willing to look at the world through someone else's lens?*

Imagine a creative supervisor of a team of ten extremely creative marketing people. The supervisor is sixty-five (but looks about fifty). The ten creative salespeople are all in their twenties or early thirties. One day, the creative supervisor notices, within a span of fifteen minutes, that, at any given moment during the day, no less than three different direct reports of his, in three different cubicles, are likely to be busy sending text messages to... who knows whom?

Personal acquaintances? Family members? Each other? He has no idea. All he knows is that, when he was getting started in the business, personal calls during working hours were forbidden, and all that time spent text-messaging seems a lot like what his manager used to call "personal calls."

So he sends out a memo: From here on out, text-messaging in the office is forbidden.

When the CEO gets wind of this, he asks for a private meeting with the manager. Has he considered that the younger people in the department might live, breathe, and eat text messages, and that they might represent important customer demographic groups the company is targeting? Is it possible that text messages are as natural and automatic a form of communication for this generation as picking up the phone, or popping into the cubicle down the hall, was (and is) for previous generations? Last but not least, will forbidding text-messaging in the office make it easier or harder to retain these creative young marketing professionals?

The next morning, the supervisor rescinds his memo, apologizes for sending it in the first place, and, during the same meeting, simply asks his team to be sure that all text messages they send are, directly or indirectly, related to them doing their jobs better. He tells them he trusts them to figure out what that boundary line is. And he thanks them for all their great work.

Sending out that memo forbidding text messages in the workplace equals *looking at the workplace through your own lens.*

Admitting you made a mistake, reversing it, and telling your people you trust them to do their job in the way that feels most right to them *equals looking at the workplace through someone else's lens.*

There are, no doubt, dozens, hundreds, even thousands of other my lens/your lens examples we could look at, but you get the idea.

THE REALITY: YOU NEED TO ATTRACT AND RETAIN CREATIVE, ENGAGED PEOPLE

"Turned on" people figure out how to beat the competition. "Turned off" people only complain about being beaten by the competition."

— BEN SIMONTON, Author, Leading People To Be Highly Motivated And Committed

As the economy improves, the competition for the most creative workers (the ones that everybody wants) will become more demanding than ever. These innovative knowledge workers will determine the fates of whole companies—and whole industries! Regardless of what is happening in the rest of the job market, these workers will always have attractive options before them. The question is: Will you be ready to do what it takes to attract and retain them?

To do that, I believe, you must move beyond some conventional assumptions about the design, look, and feel of your workplace. For most of our history, workplace designers have assumed that all or most of organizations' employees are essentially identical. Designing a working space for one person in a given department meant designing the workspace for the entire department. This book, as I have said, charts a very different approach: one of tailoring the workplace to the needs of the knowledge workers.

If the idea of matching tools and workspaces to individual employee needs sounds troublesome, or expensive, or time-consuming to you, you are certainly not alone. Yet, before you opt to make the same decisions (and get the same results) that most organizations do when addressing these questions, consider the generational groupings of the various people who now work for your organization.

All of us, regardless of our age, now have a remarkable and

unprecedented "cross-pollination" opportunity to interact with FIVE working generations at the same time, each speaking its own distinctive language, each having unique needs and work styles. They are: Traditionalists, Baby Boomers, Generation X, Millennials, and Generation 2020.

Beware! Treating these five groups as identical as you plan or upgrade your organization's workspaces can cost you and your enterprise dearly in terms of employee attraction, retention, productivity, and competitive advantage.

THE WORKPLACE GENERATIONS: TRADITIONALISTS

"A sense of personal responsibility and a commitment to honesty is characteristic of this generation. Those were values bred into the young men and women coming of age at the time the war [World War II] broke out. It's how they were raised."

— **WESLEY KO**,
World War II Veteran

Meet the oldest of the five workplace generations: the Traditionalists, the workers born before 1946. These workers—many of whom are working into their seventies and eighties—lived through the Great Depression, World War II, and the Korean War. Their primary values are DEPENDABILITY and SACRIFICE. They are willing to put aside individual goals and aspirations for the good of the group. They are big on discipline, team play, and respect for authority. They tend be conservative or even pessimistic, and strive to think in the long term. They are the most resistant of the five generations to new forms of communication technology.

Traditionalists, like Baby Boomers, are often seen by younger workers as "digital immigrants" because they did not grow up speaking the language of a digital world. To offer only the most obvious example, most Traditionalists took their time embracing twenty-first-century social media forums. A fair number are of them still holding out against this powerful medium, which is now second nature, and a potentially important workplace resource, to millions of younger workers.

KEY TAKEAWAY: To work effectively with Traditionalists, you should be prepared to appeal to the common good.

THE WORKPLACE GENERATIONS: THE BABY BOOMERS

"The Boomers' biggest impact will be on eliminating the term 'retirement' and inventing a new stage of life... the new career arc."

— ROSABETH MOSS KANTER

The second-oldest of the five workplace generations: the Baby Boomers, the workers born between 1946 and 1964. This large group includes most of the major decision makers who will be calling the shots between now and 2030. Their primary values are CHALLENGING LIMITS and QUESTIONING EVERYTHING. Baby Boomers are willing to confront authority when and as circumstances require, and they tend to have a stronger sense of social responsibility and a deeper understanding of the need for change and reform than the Traditionalists (those workers born before 1946). They are, as a rule, profoundly optimistic and willing to believe that any worthy goal can be achieved. They're generally less formal than Traditionalists, and they are more likely to focus on their own individual career goals than on team initiatives. They are generally receptive to new communication technologies, although Baby Boomers, like Traditionalists, are often seen by younger workers as digital immigrants. This is because the Boomers did not grow up speaking the language of a digital world. For instance, some Boomers took their time embracing twenty-first-century social media forums like Facebook and Twitter. Most of them have now adopted this massively important medium, which is hardwired into the younger half of the workforce.

KEY TAKEAWAY: To work efficiently with Baby Boomers, you should be prepared to identify a new and exciting goal that has not been attained before.

THE WORKPLACE GENERATIONS: GENERATION X

"We're the middle children of history... no purpose or place. We have no Great War, no Great Depression. Our great war is a spiritual war. Our great depression is our lives."

— From the movie Fight Club

"We watched our parents remain loyal to a company/lifestyle/job only to be miserable at the end. Our strategy is to find a position that blends our family/work/life into a cohesive entity that satisfies the monetary bank account and our karmic bank account."

— Anonymous Gen-X Internet

The group known as Generation X comprises workers born between 1965 and 1976. More cynical than any of the other four groups, these workers are likely to have little or no initial loyalty to the company they work for. Their primary value is INDEPENDENCE. More than any other modern generation, their world is likely to be built around the concept of "looking out for number one." They expect to change jobs frequently and are deeply wary of promises made by authority figures. They are comfortable with multiple communication technologies, and they adapt to new media platforms fairly easily. In any situation, they are likely to want to know "what's in it for me." They are much more interested in short-term outcomes than in long-term outcomes.

KEY TAKEAWAY: To work effectively with members of this group, you must be able to prove to each individual Gen-Xer that you are worth his/her valuable time, attention, and/or money.

THE WORKPLACE GENERATIONS: THE MILLENNIALS

"More than 85% of hiring managers and human-resource executives said they feel that Millennials have a stronger sense

*of entitlement than older workers, according to a survey by
CareerBuilder.com. The generation's greatest expectations:
higher pay (74% of respondents); flexible work schedules
(61%); a promotion within a year (56%);
and more vacation or personal time (50%)."*

— **RON ALSOP**, reporter and editor,
The Wall Street Journal

Now, meet the next of the five great American workplace generations: the group known as the Millennials, whose workers were born
between 1977 and 1997. The Millennials are well educated (roughly 60% are college graduates). Their primary values are FUN and
CONNECTION. Many of these workers received significantly
more parental attention and support in their youth than the Generation X workers did.

This generation grew up with computer games, the Internet, and the
World Wide Web. They are not just comfortable with communications
technology; communications technology is an important part of their
identity. They are tolerant, energetic, and demanding. They have
extremely short attention spans, thrive on visuals, prefer collaborative
give-and-take to long lectures, and expect to see results more or less
instantly. Millennials will make up roughly 50% of the workforce

in the year 2020, which means that ignoring their priorities and communication preferences is a big, and potentially fatal, mistake for any business interesting in retaining the most creative people.

KEY TAKEAWAY: To work effectively with Millennials, you must be prepared to entertain them and provide some form of social stimulation, because their whole life is about having fun and interacting with others.

THE WORKPLACE GENERATIONS: GENERATION 2020

"An overwhelming 37% of net kids have visited an online virtual world ... and by 2015, at least 55% of all Internet kids will visit online virtual worlds for playing, socialize or meet friends according to emarketer studies... (Generation) 2020 will be the most multi-tasking generation to have ever existed, (being) perfectly comfortable with multiple information streams and activities running at the same time, having a number of browser windows open at once, chatting via Instant Messaging (with) the TV on in the background while sending messages to friends."

— Social Machinery blog

So far, we have learned about the Traditionalists, the Baby Boomers, Generation X, and the Millennials. Now meet the youngest of the five great American workplace generations, which is coming soon to a workplace near you .... Generation 2020. This highly educated generation, born around or shortly before the year 2000, will enter the workforce by the end of the present decade, during a period when many Traditionalists will likely still be quite active. Analysts are still working out what to expect from this group. Words that are being used now to describe their values include:

Connected. Expect this group to be even more "wired" than the Millennials, because their entire lives have been spent under the powerful influence of the World Wide Web, online video games, social media, and virtual worlds like Second Life. As you read these words, they are updating their Facebook status.

Concerned. Members of Generation 2020 appear to be the most sensitive of all the five groups to environmental problems and related social issues.

Careful. The recommendations of peers will carry enormous weight with this group. Expect these workers to think twice before making big purchase decisions. Unlike the Millennials, they are coming of age during a time of economic austerity. They are likely to seek value and be much more cautious with economic and career decisions, and thus share some important values with Traditionalists.

Collaborative. Like the Millennials, they are likely to be quite comfortable with collaborative endeavors, either face-to-face or virtual.

When in doubt, engage with these workers on Facebook—in ways that cater to their expressed tastes. Celebrate their technological prowess, which can be quite astonishing. Recently, a customer said to me, "Can you please e-mail that PowerPoint to me? I don't think I'm up to making the edits myself, but I'll have Billy help me with it." Billy was the customer's fourteen-year-old grandson! That's a perfect example of a (future) Generation 2020 worker pitching in to help out a Traditionalist. We should all get used to those kinds of examples. They show us the future of the highly effective, highly collaborative, highly productive workplace!

KEY TAKEAWAY: To work effectively with these young workers, you will be have to be prepared to understand, become part of, and respect their network. Be amazed by, and celebrate, their ability to interact within that network and accomplish things within it.

MOVING BEYOND DEMOGRAPHIC BIGOTRY

"I never did anything alone. Whatever was accomplished in this country was accomplished collectively."

— Golda Meir (1898–1978),
Fourth Prime Minister of Israel

"Before you go and criticize the younger generation, just remember who raised them."

— Anonymous

If you're like most company owners, founders, CEOs, and senior executives I've worked with, when you heard about the five generations that will be converging simultaneously on the workplace in the year 2020, you thought, "This is a big change. I want our organization to be on the right side of this change."

Congratulations! You have taken the first step: Recognition.

The initial, and perhaps most essential, step is simply recognizing that the workplace marked by the familiar two-generation dynamic we have all seen in the movies (older vs. younger, senior vs. junior, experienced vs. inexperienced) has been obsolete for decades. As one of my younger coworkers put it recently, fixating on two generations in the workplace, on a generational contest that one group wins and another group loses, is "so last century" that it's not worth the effort.

The critical step to building a workplace for *this* century is recognizing that many of our assumptions about what the workplace should look like, feel like, and be like are based on that old dynamic. We must accept that big changes are inevitable if we want our organizations to attract and retain the very best people.

The change I am talking about is not imminent. It is *underway* right now, today, as you read these words.

Some companies—I have profiled a number of them in this book—have learned how to make sense of the current four-generation workplace, and are well positioned to remain competitive in a five-generation environment. All of those companies, as you will see, share one important common trait: They create and support a workplace with no room for demographic bigotry.

That means no shutting out a generation because you don't happen to be a part of it. That means no dismissing people because of their age, their perceived relevance, or their perceived level of experience. In the 2020 workspace, the workspace that is part of the revolution about which I am writing in this book, every generation has something to contribute. Organizations that don't recognize that lose out, both in the marketplace and in the workplace.

CLOSER TO BULLETPROOF

*"If you do not raise your eyes you will think
that you are the highest point."*
— **ANTONIO PORCHI**a (1885–1968),
Italian-born Argentinian poet

Today, no organization can afford the kind of generational isolation in which employees put themselves in a single generational box, and allow themselves to see only the confines of their own box. The generational isolation I am talking about here means:

- Getting all your counsel and advice only from people within your generation.

- Only spending time with friends and associates who come from your generational group.

- Reading and listening only to people from your generation.

- Ignoring other generational input, or even any involvement with them.

My wife's father, a very wise man, was a top executive with the Federal Deposit Insurance Corporation for many years. He would refer to this kind of activity in people groups as "people pooling their ignorance." Without the vigorous, continuous exchange of generational insights, we are likely to be blinded by our own myopic, one-dimensional generational vision.

Organizationally speaking, two heads are better than one ... but five heads gets you closer to bulletproof!

Mark Zuckerberg, the founder of Facebook, recently became the world's youngest billionaire. Do you imagine the venture capitalists with whom he worked to finance his company looked down on him because he was a Millennial? Because he had different communication preferences than they did? Because he saw things differently than they did? It was because Zuckerberg and his investors brought different perspectives and different approaches to the project that they were valuable to each other.

Here are the key ingredients of an organization that has waged and won the Great Workplace Revolution: Demographic diversity, demographic acceptance, demographic respect, and demographic communication. *Not* demographic bigotry. We can no longer afford that!

"WHAT'S IN IT FOR ME?"...
or "WHAT'S IN IT FOR US?"

"If everyone is moving forward together,
then success takes care of itself."

— **HENRY FORD** (1863–1947),
American industrialist

These days, lots of workers are looking for a way to become more indispensable to—and thus less likely to be laid off by—their current employers. By the same token, lots of job-seekers are looking to stand out from the pack in the tightest job market in years. Herein lies an opportunity.

As you have seen, five very different working generations will somehow have to learn to collaborate successfully in order to survive and thrive. This unprecedented state of affairs leads to a great opening for workers who wish to prove their value over time ... and job-seekers who wish to stand out from the ever-larger pack of competing applicants. Become a generational interpreter.

Here's an example of what I mean. Let's say you're fifty-five years old. That makes you a Baby Boomer. Over the next decade, Baby

Boomers who can prove their ability to truly communicate effectively with all four of the other workplace generations—Traditionalists, Generation X, Millennials, and the newest workplace group, Generation 2020—will be extremely valuable contributors to their organization. That means it is in your best interests to determine how each of these groups is likely to approach the critical question "What's in it for me?" in regard to any new organizational initiative… and help members of each of these groups communicate with each other effectively and create effective coalitions.

I'm often asked what I think the most critical workplace skill is likely to be for knowledge workers over the next decade. Here's my answer: The ability to understand, translate, build bridges, and build coalitions across generational lines. I call this "generational coaching."

Workers who demonstrate their ability to do this—either in their current positions or in new ones—will be the most sought-after contributors of all over the next few years. Let's look now at some additional strategies for communicating effectively on the job with members of each of the five demographic groups. What follows is a brief but reliable summary of how to interact effectively with, and build alliances with, members of each group. This alliance-building skill is,

I believe, the critical skill gap that organizations will need to fill over the next few decades.

To engage with and build alliances with TRADITIONALISTS: Respect their privacy, respect their personal space, respect their possessions (as in, don't touch those possessions without permission), and last but not least, respect their personal status. If possible, schedule a meeting with them in their personal office or work area. Stress the importance of order, continuity, and fulfilling responsibilities.

To engage with and build alliances with BABY BOOMERS: Stay after hours, help out with an overdue project, and find some work-related topic that will help to give this person a competitive advantage over others in the workspace. Baby Boomers are the original workaholics, and many of them are extremely competitive.

To engage with and build alliances with GENERATION X: Be prepared to use e-mail or text messages as your primary communication tool. Keep the messages short, and keep them coming. Appeal directly to this worker's personal interests; organizational loyalty is only likely to exist to the degree that is directly supports a Gen Xer's short-term goals.

To engage with and build alliances with MILLENNIALS: Be

prepared to use e-mail or text messages as your primary communication tool. Keep the messages *incredibly* short, and keep them coming. Talk about what's happening outside of this person's working life. If at all possible, meet and connect before or after hours in a non-work environment. Work/life balance is a critical issue for members of this generation.

To engage with and build alliances with GENERATION 2020: Emphasize group activities and networking opportunities. Participate in group activities, both inside and outside the workplace. If you make the discussion fun, you will be on this person's radar screen; if you don't, you won't. Appeal to this worker's sense of fun and play, and to social causes that he or she believes in. Learn what social media portals this person favors—it may be a new one you've never heard of—and adopt it as your own.

DIALOGUE AND DEBATE

"Many ideas grow better when transplanted into another mind than the one where they sprang up."
—OLIVER WENDELL HOLMES, SR.

I am sometimes asked to simplify or summarize my position on the five very different generational groups who will be occupying the American workplace from the year 2020 onward. Typically, the request for simplification comes from one of two groups. It either comes from people who have a hard time getting their heads around the complexity of the topic (and I can't blame them!) or it comes from people who dismiss the idea of important generational workplace differences existing in the first place. I respect both groups, of course, and I believe I have come up with a single "generational manifesto" sentence that is simple and straightforward enough for busy people in the first group to understand and remember, and relevant enough to the discussion for skeptical people in the second group to accept.

My generational manifesto: CHOOSE DIALOGUE, COLLABORATION, AND DEBATE OVER COMMAND AND CONTROL.

That's the "big generational idea" for the twenty-first-century workplace. That single idea is the one you will want to bear in mind above all others as you create your organization's workplace strategy for the next decades.

We can all, I think, agree with a strategy that divides the multigenerational workplace into two instantly, intuitively recognizable groups: the "Digital Immigrants" who did not grow up with easy access to computer-supported social interaction (the Traditionalists and the Baby Boomers) and the "Digital Natives" who did (Generation X, Millennials, and Generation 2020). That difference in upbringing, I believe, carries huge workplace implications.

For reasons that have a great deal to do with the vast digital divide, workers in the first group are, as a general but very reliable rule, more comfortable accepting a classic, hierarchical, "command and control" workspace environment than are workers in the second group.

"Digital Immigrants" generally don't have a problem accepting the idea of a big corner office for the CEO or founder. For better or for worse, they're used to getting instructions from that office. "Digital Natives," on the other hand—who are all about instant collaboration, easy access, and quick response—are more likely to have problems adapting to a physical environment built around the idea of supporting a top-down management structure.

Younger workers, regardless of the names we assign to their various age groups, can be expected to have less patience with traditional "do it because the boss said so" initiatives and assignments. Thanks to powerful influences like Facebook, instant messaging, and video games, these workers expect more in the way of collaboration, communication, stimulus, entertainment, and, yes, emotional support from the workplace than their counterparts who were born before about 1964.

If you expect to build a workplace that supports a "command and control" workspace philosophy, don't expect to get the best from, or retain, creative workers born after, say, the Beatles' first appearance on the Ed Sullivan Show. That was February, 1964.

If you don't remember Beatlemania, there's a very good chance that you spend more time on Facebook than I do, are more likely to do your best work in groups of three or more than I am, are more likely to reach out to people with differing work responsibilities than I am, and are more comfortable bouncing your ideas off of people by means of digital media than I am. You are also more likely to push back when a supervisor shares an idea that you think is flawed, and God bless you for that.

None of this is meant to suggest that your unique set of ways of working are right and someone else's are wrong. This does mean, though, that, as we design a workspace that gets the best from everyone, we need to remember that the workplaces many older workers came from would probably bore younger workers to death... and wouldn't inspire them to stick around!

CONNECTING THE DOTS

"Alone we can do so little;
together we can do so much."

— **HELEN KELLER** (1880–1968),
American author, political activist, and lecturer

So: Why should employers facing tough economic challenges bother learning, investing in, or implementing any of this? Why build your organization around the ideas you've just read, or the ones in the next section? It's not as if there has been a shortage of people writing about the emergence of a cross-generational workforce. What there has been a shortage of is good advice on how best to CONNECT THE DOTS by creating and sustaining a workforce that engages and retains the most talented Traditionalists, Baby Boomers, Gen Xers, Millennials, and members of Generation 2020.

There are twelve essential strategies you can follow to win the cream of the crop from all five of these generations and engage them in your organization's cause. To implement these strategies is to connect the dots—to take practical action on what would otherwise be little more than academic information.

> Success in today's marketplace requires that there be *one* person whose job it is to take the initiative, start connecting these dots, and start evangelizing for a great workplace on behalf of the rest of the enterprise!

I invite *you* to become that person—to accept that personal challenge, to commit to learning more each and every day about how your organization can benefit from the twelve core strategies—to join The Great Workplace Revolution, a revolution where everybody wins! How? By becoming your organization's Great Workplace Revolution Coach!

BUILDING A COALITION FOR CHANGE: THE GREAT WORKPLACE REVOLUTION COACH

"The lightning spark of thought generated in the solitary mind awakens its likeness in another mind."

— **THOMAS CARLYLE** (1795–1881),
Scottish essayist, satirist, and historian

It's time to get started.

Our first and perhaps most important responsibility is to identify the "point person" who will assume the job of building and supporting a powerful coalition for change in the workplace. I call this person the Great Place To Work Coach, or Great Workplace Revolution Coach for short. From this point forward in the book, I'm going to assume that you, the reader, are that Great Workplace Revolution Coach, and that you are interested not only in creating a great workplace with plenty of opportunity for yourself—the classic "what's in it for me" outlook—but that you also have a certain sense of mission for the organization as a whole. I am going to assume that you believe in making things happen that benefit everyone you come in contact with during the course of the working day. To a considerable extent, The Great Workplace Revolution is a matter of moving from "What's in it for me?" to "What's in it for us?" As Great Workplace Revolution Coach, you will need to be a role model who supports everyone in the organization, high or low, Traditionalist or Generation 2020, to make that transition.

So, how do you pull that off? By sharing, and living, great examples. At various points in this book, you'll be reading true accounts of how companies large and small have reaped huge bottom-line benefits, and established un-reproducible rapport with incredibly loyal segments of the marketplace, by building Great Places to Work. These companies include firms you've heard of like Zappos, Southwest Airlines, and the Walt Disney Companies, as well as outfits you may not have heard of, like Blue Book Services, The Land of Nod, and Building Services, Inc. Whatever their industry, whatever their target customer, whatever their level of market penetration, these enterprises always share one important common element in their company history. At some point, someone in senior management, very often a company founder, assumed the role of Great Workplace Revolution Coach (even without assuming that specific name). At some point, that person made creating and sustaining an employee-focused organization a top priority for the entire enterprise.

This fateful decision, which can come at any stage of a business's development, launches nothing short of an internal, ongoing Great Place to Work Revolution, a revolution driven and supported over time by two critical factors. The first of these factors is a tangible, practical concern for the bottom line in both the short and long terms. The companies we are discussing are eager to create the kind of enduring market advantage that enables their enterprise not only to survive during periods of economic downturn, but actually to thrive and expand during these periods. Take a look at the histories of the companies I have profiled in this book, and you will see that many of them have, in fact, secured this coveted degree of loyalty from their customers: When times are tough, their customers rely on them more, not less.

Successful revolutions, however, are not waged on behalf of numbers, even numbers that demonstrate a company's ability to thrive during a recession. They are waged on behalf of specific values that overcome the inevitable complacency, turf wars, and petty rivalries that crop up in any organization. These values are the second factor that drive and expand the organization's Great Place to Work movement. By definition, these values come from, and are modeled by, top management. Interestingly, the values that drive a successful Great Workplace Revolution may be expressed in many different forms, depending on the culture of the company, but they always touch on some or all of my twelve essential strategies for creating a great place to work.

Let's take another look at those twelve strategies now and, briefly, at how they have been applied at our company, Thomas Interior Systems. The list, as well as a short self-observation piece from our side (set in parentheses), appears below.

1. Identify the organization's core values and talk about those values frequently with customers and employees. These are the customer-focused values you will hire employees for, and fire employees for, if they consistently deviate from those values. You'll learn more about developing this list of values in the next section of this book. (At our company, we post our values publicly and prominently. You can't help seeing them the moment you walk into our reception area. What's more, we base our whole review system on a self-review against those same core values, and we make a point of talking about the values regularly at team meetings.)

2. Design and constantly refine a truly creative work space based on direct employee feedback. You will know you have designed this kind of workspace when it becomes a recruiting tool for your organization. Your physical workplace must attract and retain creative problem-solvers and people who care, and must be based on their best ideas. (Each team member's working environment is based on direct engagement with that employee to find out exactly what he or she needs to do the job.)

3. Put the right person in the right job. This is your organization's responsibility! Personality, work style, and problem-solving assessments can be a great resource for fulfilling this responsibility.

Remember: Every employee "failure" is really a failure of your organization's hiring and human resource processes, not a failure of the individual in question! (We have built our entire human resource process around the objective of finding both the right person and the right fit, based on each employee's distinctive conative profile, as determined by the superb assessment systems of Kolbe Corp. Don't worry if the word "conative" sounds unfamiliar to you right now; you'll be learning more about this in the next section of the book.)

4. Provide constant accommodation to, and understanding of, the whole employee. This means, for instance, understanding that you've really hired not just one person, but that person's whole family. To use just one example, consider the fact that the ability to bring a child and/or family member to work dramatically increases an employee's pride in his or her job. The result: Greater buy-in to the mission, deeper loyalty to the company, and more intense commitment to the customer. Other examples of understanding and adapting to the whole employee include: flex time, shift-swapping, extended leave when it's necessary, and so forth. (We encourage people to bring relatives into the workplace from time to time because we know that whenever we hire someone, we are not just hiring an individual, but an entire family. We also schedule mandatory "listening time," in either one-on-one or small group sessions, so that supervisors can hear first-hand about what is going on in people's lives and how they feel about working for our company.)

5. *Build into the culture appropriate recognition for a job well done.* "Recognition tools" like thank-you cards and note cards for colleagues (as well as for customers and vendors) need to become a part of your organization's daily life. These should reflect authentic gratitude for any, and every, job well done. "Most Valuable Player" awards promote an "all crew and no passenger" workplace philosophy, and that philosophy, which I'll be exploring in much greater depth later on in the book, ultimately helps the customer. (We have special thank-you cards that we use to acknowledge great work; most people choose to display them in their work spaces as badges of honor! That's not mandatory, though. We give people choices about how they prefer to receive recognition for a job well done.)

6. *Support a truly collaborative workplace, both physically and emotionally.* This means providing resources and person-to-person support that promotes problem-solving, quality improvement, brainstorming, think tanks, and effective post-mortems whenever a project concludes. (Our work space is designed to bring people together and make them feel good about interacting with one another. That

means learning spaces, team spaces, collaboration spaces, fun spaces, and, yes, private spaces for when you feel you need a break!)

7. *Appoint someone Director of Fun.* Whether this is a full-time position or on addition to someone's current list of responsibilities isn't important. What's important is that your team members see, and experience first-hand, the positive experience they are supposed to deliver to the customer. Your Director of Fun must find new reasons to celebrate and new ways to enhance enjoyment of the job! (Our Director of Fun now has a committee of five to work with... although she is still in charge of, and personally responsible for, this important responsibility!)

8. *Create after-work events that involve direct personal contact with customers and employees.* This kind of event amounts to a fun, collaborative team effort to improve all aspects of customer service. (Our most popular after-work events with customers include music and sports events at Chicago's United Center, where our company has a private box. These events give us a great chance to spend time with customers, and they are also great team-building opportunities.)

9. *Give something back to the community.* Doing this as a group improves team cohesion, gives you a great PR opportunity, and helps customers understand your values. (Our company's team-building

activities in this area include campaigns that get food out to homeless people and help needy families with their holiday shopping.)

10. Ensure that each employee's work space makes good ergonomic sense. This reduces stress, improves morale, and improves the quality of our interactions with customers (and everyone else)! (If you work for us, your work environment gets a Health Fitup—an annual ergonomic review—at least once a year.)

11. Invest in ongoing education and personal development. This is not an "added expense." It's an investment that pays off for everyone. (This ongoing learning takes place through two venues: Thomas University, where we conduct courses for employees on finance, exercise training, and all kinds of other topics—and in the Thomas Learning Center, where the focus is on building up work-related skills.)

12. Give employees regular feedback. Recommended evaluation time: every six months. In terms of determining whom to hold on to and whom to reassign or part company with, your goal should be to evaluate employees against your organization's core values first, and then against specific performance metrics second. (This strategy brings the process full circle. Our employee evaluation process takes place every six months and is designed, as noted above, around a self-review based on the company's core values, followed by the supervisor's feedback within the same core value areas. Then we look at the performance metrics. Because we want the communication to be a two-way conversation, we also ask for feedback by posing three important questions: *What's working? What's not? What's your great idea?*)

Please bear in mind that these twelve strategies are a starting point for ongoing, *daily* organizational reinvention—not a checklist you complete once, put away, then pull out and review every year!

HOW MANY OF THE TWELVE STRATEGIES ARE "THE WAY YOU DO THINGS" RIGHT NOW?

"Values are not just words, values are what we live by. They're about the causes that we champion and the people we fight for."
— Senator John Kerry

The list of strategies you've just read must become "the way we do things here" for each and every employee in your organization. They must be imbedded in your long-term and short-term planning. They must be the foundation of your customer service strategy, because no meaningful and sustainable improvements in customer service are possible without them. Last but not least, they must also become the means by which you listen to the sounds of the workplace.

To perfect the neglected art of listening your own workplace, you must, as Great Workplace Coach, be willing to put your own employees first on the daily priority list. Yes, you read right: To win this Great Workplace Revolution, you must find a way to get beyond all the familiar clichés you've heard about putting the customer first, or the stockholders first, or anyone else in the world first, on your company's priority list. Those clichés are mistaken. You must consistently, unambiguously, and joyfully put your own employees first in your enterprise, because that is the only possible way for you to take care of customers, shareholders, stakeholders, or anyone else on your list. As my good friend Shep Hyken, author of *The Amazement Revolution,* put it recently: "When you build a company around the idea of taking care of employees, taking care of customers becomes easier for everyone."

Here is my single favorite quote on this important topic, which comes from the legendary former CEO of Southwest Airlines, Herb Kelleher: "Years ago, business gurus used to apply the business school conundrum to me: 'Who comes first? Your shareholders, your employees, or your customers?' I said, 'Well, that's easy,' but my response was heresy at that time. I said employees come first and if employees are treated right, they treat the outside world right, the outside world uses the company's product again, and that makes the shareholders happy. That really is the way that it works, and it's not a conundrum at all."

Any problem you are having with your customers—and I do mean literally *any* problem—has as its root cause some problem you are having with one or more employees (possibly you). Some organizations don't feel comfortable acknowledging that reality directly, but that doesn't make it any less true. You cannot just throw a seminar at your team and expect problems with customers to disappear overnight. You must *change the way people feel about going to work.* This is why learning to listen to your workplace is so vitally important! If you know something's wrong within your organization, but you can't say precisely what it is, the odds are good that what you are "hearing" is the sound of one or more of these twelve strategies being ignored by someone in authority in your enterprise. You must fix that problem before you attempt to fix anything else!

So: Which of the twelve strategies is causing your enterprise difficulty right now—*because it is being ignored or minimized?* Is it one you and your enterprise have been able to rely on in the past as an organizational strength? Is it rooted in some known best practices that you've simply lost sight of? Or is it a strategy that you have previously targeted for improvement, a strategy that needs some creativity, experimentation, and assessment to become part of How We Do Things Around Here?

A little later on in the book, I'll give you an assessment exercise that will help you identify where you have strengths you can leverage, and where there may be room for improvement. If you are leading the Great Workplace Revolution effort, you will need to know this!

THE COACH'S BIGGEST AND MOST IMPORTANT JOB: UNDERSTAND THE VALUES

"Effectiveness without values is a tool without a purpose."
— **EDWARD DE BONO**,
physician, author, inventor, consultant

The role of the Great Workplace Revolution Coach—whether that individual is the founder of the company, a senior employee who has formally retired but who has come back to play the role of facilitator, or a senior executive who is ready to lead the Great Workplace Revolution—is to identify the values that support the organization's mission.

These values are much more than the concise mission statement that sums up the enterprise's purpose. Your organization's values must be a snapshot of the best and most supportive motivators actually used by the people who come to work each day.

The values you identify, circulate, and refer back to on a daily basis must derive from the model day-to-day operations of your organization. These are the beliefs, attitudes, and core assumptions that make it possible for others to join the Great Workplace Revolution Coach in building a superb place to work. But first, the Coach must identify those values!

If you are the Great Workplace Revolution Coach, your values must not only be the core motivators and assumptions you wish other people would adopt, but also the core motivators and assumptions you yourself are personally willing to model to each and every member of the organization, on a daily basis, during every single interaction!

That's a tall order, one that's worth considering closely before taking on the role of Great Workplace Revolution Coach. After all, if you define the core organizational value of respect, and then say something rude to someone who reports to you, the entire organization is likely to refuse to buy into the values you identify!

This is why I emphasize the idea of noticing the most supportive values that are already driving your organization, rather than trying to identify some hypothetical list of ideal values that people (including you) may or may not be willing to buy into. Most organizations go about this task in the wrong order: They try to impose a set of ideal values on an existing workforce that has no reason to accept them.

Identifying the values is the essential first strategy item on my list of twelve actions your organization must take consistently in order to create and sustain a great place to work. In the next part of the book, we'll take an in-depth look at all twelve, and share some essential takeaways for the Great Workplace Revolution Coach relating to each strategy. But first...

DO A SELF-ASSESSMENT: WHERE ARE YOU RIGHT NOW?

"You never find yourself until you face the truth."
— **PEARL BAILEY** (1918–1990),
American singer and actress

I'd like you to look once again at the twelve essential strategies for creating a great place to work. In the space below each item, rate your own company on a scale of zero to ten, with zero meaning you have taken no action in this area, and ten meaning you have evidence that you are an industry role model in deploying that strategy. Find out where you stand!

1. Identifying the organization's core values, and talking about those values frequently with customers and employees.

   0 1 2 3 4 5 6 7 8 9 10

   No action Industry Role Model

2. Designing and refining a creative work space.

   0 1 2 3 4 5 6 7 8 9 10

   No action Industry Role Model

3. Putting the right person in the right job.

   0 1 2 3 4 5 6 7 8 9 10

   No action Industry Role Model

4. Providing constant accommodation to, and understanding of, the whole employee.

   0 1 2 3 4 5 6 7 8 9 10

   No action Industry Role Model

5. Building into the culture appropriate recognition for a job well done.

   0 1 2 3 4 5 6 7 8 9 10

No action Industry Role Model

6. Supporting a truly collaborative workplace, both physically and emotionally.

0 1 2 3 4 5 6 7 8 9 10

No action Industry Role Model

7. Appointing someone Director of Fun.

0 1 2 3 4 5 6 7 8 9 10

No action Industry Role Model

8. Creating after-work events that involve direct personal contact with customers and employees.

0 1 2 3 4 5 6 7 8 9 10

No action Industry Role Model

9. Giving something back to the community.

0 1 2 3 4 5 6 7 8 9 10

No action Industry Role Model

10. Ensuring that each employee's work space makes good ergonomic sense.

0 1 2 3 4 5 6 7 8 9 10

No action Industry Role Model

11. Investing in ongoing education and personal development.

0   1   2   3   4   5   6   7   8   9   10

No action Industry Role Model

12. Giving employees regular feedback.

0   1   2   3   4   5   6   7   8   9   10

No action Industry Role Model

Did you finish the self-assessment? Great! Now, let's put what you've learned to work.

Of the twelve Great Workplace Revolution strategies, which ONE would you say is your organization's current strong suit? Write your answer below, as well as a sentence or two explaining why you feel that way. Give specific examples.

_____

_____

_____

This is the strategy you will want to "talk up" regularly in team meetings, and offer appropriate positive reinforcement and recognition for it, whenever and wherever you see it.

Of the twelve Great Workplace Revolution strategies, which ONE would you say is currently your organization's weakest link? Write your answer below, as well as a sentence or two explaining why you feel that way.

_____

_____

_____

This is the strategy you will want to mention frequently to senior management at your organization as most deserving of work or, if you are the senior management, the strategy you will want to make improving a high personal and organizational priority. This doesn't necessarily mean you need to spend large amounts of money developing this particular strategy, but you should be ready, willing, and able to invest resources like time, energy, and attention to developing proficiency in this strategy.

As Great Workplace Revolution Coach, you should know, and be ready to discuss at any moment, the one strategy that is your organization's strong suit ...as well as the one strategy that you are most committed to improving. They will change over time. Make this a never-ending process!

It's time to move on to Part Three of the book, in which we look at each of the twelve strategies in much more detail. Don't stop here... keep up the momentum!

PART THREE:
THE TWELVE STRATEGIES, IN DEPTH

LAUNCHING AN ONGOING REVOLUTION

"We are what we repeatedly do.
Excellence, therefore, is not an act, but a habit."

— **ARISTOTLE**, Greek philosopher and scientist

Please forgive me for repeating this point, but it is so important that I feel I have to open this next section of the book with it: The job of building a Great Place to Work is never complete! Your aim as Great Workplace Revolution Coach is to create an "unfinished masterpiece" workplace, one that is always dynamic, always evolving, always adapting to new people, situations, and opportunities.

It's time to start creating a whole new organization, based on where you are right now, using what you have in front of you as of this moment. As you begin this essential task of transformation—by learning more about how to implement the twelve strategies I shared with you in Part One of this book—I would ask, first and foremost, that you not get too distracted by the various labels I've attached to the twelve ideas you will be looking at in depth. You can call these actions by whatever names you want. What's important is not what you call them, but that you actually do them!

It is by executing these twelve essential strategies—whether you have a lot of money to work with or no money at all, whether you have fifteen minutes a day to devote to these ideas or all the time in the world—that you will launch a Great Workplace Revolution within your enterprise, and begin the critical ongoing work that will allow that Revolution to endure over time.

Why bother? Because your organization's success in the marketplace depends on total commitment to this revolution. In fact, I believe that implementing what you are about to learn is more important than any other change or process improvement you may implement within a team. I say this based on long decades of personal experience, in the form of direct engagement with countless enterprises (including, of course, my own). I have reached the conclusion that any seemingly positive short-term change we may achieve "on the ground" within our organizations—whether it involves strategic planning, product development, operations, personnel, sales, customer service, or any other area of your business you care to name—is essentially useless if we don't find some way to lock in our progress over the long term. That means making whatever short-term improvement we have achieved part of our enduring organizational culture... and that, in turn, means taking responsibility for how our people feel about showing up for work each day.

These twelve strategies are all about locking in positive change, not for the short term, but for the long term, based on the attitudes and assumptions people have about what it's like to work for our organization. These twelve ongoing assignments for organizational change and growth are all about the attitude people reinforce, either individually or in groups, about what it means to show up for work day after day. If these strategies are not implemented from the very top of the organization, we can have no realistic expectation that any positive change we make will stick around for any length of time. Once these ideas are endorsed from the top, and are tirelessly reinforced through every part of the enterprise until they become the cultural norms by which we solve problems, brainstorm ideas, and achieve meaningful goals, success in both the short and long terms becomes our direction!

Great Workplace Revolution Strategy #1: Identify the organization's core values and talk about those values frequently with customers and employees.

KEY CONCEPT: Agreeing on and maintaining core values means more to your organization than setting up rules and regulations and punishing people for violating them.

Case Study for Values that Summon the Best from Your Team: Zappos

"Businesses often forget about the culture, and ultimately they suffer for it because you can't deliver good service from unhappy employees."

— **TONY HSIEH**, CEO, Zappos

I didn't have to think long to come up with my lead role model in the area of establishing business values. Zappos, the mammoth online shoe, apparel, and accessories retailer, was (and remains) the standard-bearer for any business that aims to build people-first values into its day-to-day culture.

It's no coincidence, I believe, that the company that has been most visible in the area of championing core values is also one of the most successful and fastest-growing retailers in our wired economy. A decade ago, Zappos had virtually no revenues; today, it posts over $1 billion annually in gross merchandise sales.

Do the company's now-famous core values have something to do with that extraordinary record of success? Well, Zappos CEO Tony Hsieh thinks so, although he is quick to point out that the current list of Zappos values were only formalized seven years into the company's extraordinary history. They were committed to paper at a time when Hsieh was trying to figure out the best way to make hiring decisions on a large scale that would support the company's rapid growth. The process by which he finalized his company's list of values began as a recruitment tool; it is now the compass that guides Zappos in everything it does. I believe the values Hsieh identified are indeed root causes of the company's success, even though they were not finalized for some years. Why? Because the values Hsieh wrote down were simply reflections of values that he and his best employees already shared.

In my view, the route Hsieh followed—identifying existing values that were already present among key employees—is far preferable to the more common approach most companies follow. Most companies attempt to identify "ideal" values that may have nothing whatsoever to do with the success your company has already achieved. These ideal values might as well be a press release. They are very often dismissed by customers and employees alike as divorced from reality and essentially meaningless, and rightfully so. I would advise that you use the same process Hsieh did to create a set of real-world values that mirrors what is already making your best employees, and your best customers, happy about your organization. Tony describes that process as follows:

> "Someone from our legal department suggested that we come
> up with a list of core values to serve as a guide for managers
> to make hiring decisions. I thought about all the employees I
> wanted to clone because they represented the Zappos culture
> well, and tried to figure out what values they personified. I
> also thought about all the employees and ex-employees who

were not culture fits, and tried to figure out where there was a values disconnect. As I started creating the list, I realized that I needed to get everyone's input on what our core values should be. Over the course of a year, I emailed the entire company several times and got a lot of suggestions and feedback on which core values were the most important to our employees." ("How Zappos Infuses Culture Using Core Values," Harvard Business Review blog, May 24, 2010.)

Notice that the list was the result of an extended conversation involving Zappos senior management and its own employees. And "extended" is definitely the operative word here. It took more than a year to get it right! Hsieh knew what he was doing, however. The resulting list of "committable core values" not only aids decision-making at all levels of the organization, but also serves as the bedrock justification for hiring—or, for that matter, firing—any employee. Living up to these core values is part of the Zappos job description!

Take a look at the list Hsieh and the Zappos team eventually came up with, and see if you don't agree that that year-long conversation was time well spent.

ZAPPOS.COM'S 10 CORE VALUES

1. Deliver WOW Through Service

2. Embrace and Drive Change

3. Create Fun and A Little Weirdness

4. Be Adventurous, Creative, and Open-Minded

5. Pursue Growth and Learning

6. Build Open and Honest Relationships With Communication

7. Build a Positive Team and Family Spirit

8. Do More With Less

9. Be Passionate and Determined

10. Be Humble

Identifying, quantifying, and reinforcing the very best values your organization is already following takes a little longer than identifying a group of buzzwords that sound good, and then calling those your values ... but the more time-consuming approach has the advantage of being something you can actually implement with your existing workforce!

Hsieh liked the list of Zappos core values so much that he decided to identify them, not only as hiring values, but also as firing values! In other words, possessing all of these values dramatically increased your likelihood of being hired into some part of Zappos as it expanded, even if you had little or no technical knowledge in a given area... and subverting one or more of these values meant you increased the likelihood of your being fired from Zappos, regardless of your past contributions!

As you may have noticed, Hsieh's approach worked pretty well. Zappos is today one of the most admired, respected, and imitated firms on earth. The lesson I want you to draw from this story, however, is not that Zappos's values should be your company's values, but that your process as Great Workplace Revolution Coach should mirror Hsieh's, and that you should take some time to complete the following tasks carefully and thoughtfully. Do not rush these assignments! They are your responsibility as Great Workplace Revolution Coach.

1. Look closely at your organization's hires over an extended period (say, five years).

2. Identify the specific people who have stayed with your organization for a long time, based on the quality of their contributions.

3. Get clarity on the answer to this question: What do these people have in common?

4. Write down your answers to the question in 3, above, and make sure your organization's top leadership is in agreement with you that the values you have identified are both hiring and firing values.

5. Circulate the list within your team or organization, and talk about these values at every possible opportunity, including during performance evaluations.

Takeaways for the Great Workplace Revolution Coach:

- Work with senior management, and the enterprise as a whole, to identify a list of core values. The list should reflect the values that your very best people already follow.

- Take your time.

- Engage the team as you refine and finalize the list. The final list should be the conclusion of many in-depth conversations, not a one-way "things-had-better-change-around-here" memo.

- Use the list of core values to help in day-to-day decisions ... and to confirm hiring (and firing) decisions.

Great Workplace Revolution Strategy #2: Design and constantly refine a creative work space based on direct employee feedback.

KEY CONCEPT: A workspace is not creative unless it serves the needs of the people who work in it, and inspires them to stick around and make creative contributions. That means we need to listen carefully to employees about what they feel they should have in their surroundings

Case Study for Creative Workspace Design: Blue Book Services

"It is the long history of humankind (and animal kind, too) that those who learned to collaborate and improvise most effectively have prevailed."

— CHARLES DARWIN (1809–1882), English naturalist

Blue Book Services is a 110-year-old privately owned company that is perhaps best described as the Dun and Bradstreet of the produce industry. The company's website informs the world at large that Blue Book is a "leading credit and marketing information agency" that has been serving the international wholesale produce industry since 1901, and that now serves the international wholesale lumber and forest products industry as well. Buyers, brokers, and transporters alike rely on Blue Book ratings, reports, and information to make safe, informed, and profitable business decisions.

Jim Carr, the CEO, is a good friend of mine and a client of our company. He was kind enough to allow me to interview him for this book on the subject of building a work environment that both supports creative thinking and attracts and retains the most creative people. Here's what he had to say.

"Communication is a big part of building a creative workforce," according to Jim, "and maybe the most important part. Every year, we survey our people and ask them how we're doing in certain areas that we have established as the core responsibilities of the management team. These are things like leadership, motivational communication, and so on. So we get graded on that. That's part of the communication emphasis, and it definitely is part of supporting the creative workforce. We have 51 people, working in three different functional teams, and we try to involve everyone in the discussion process.

A Building Redesign—and an Opportunity for Dialogue

"For example, when it came time to redesign our building a year and a half ago, the executive team worked with Thomas Interior Systems to put together an initial vision of what the space was going to look like. But we didn't just implement that vision from the top down. We showed it to our associates and asked them for feedback. In essence, we said, 'Here is what we are thinking, but what would you add or take away? What would you personally like to see in a redo of our office space?' We tested the vision and got some feedback.

"That discussion generated some great ideas, most of which made it into the final design. For instance, people told us they wanted special collaboration spaces, 'touchdown sites,' set up for meeting areas along a window wall. Windows owned by everyone, not just executives. That gave windows to people for collaborative meetings along the whole west exposure of the building. That said a lot about the importance of collaboration at our organization, and we built that into the final layout. Something else they asked for was a place for smaller meetings. We heard that and liked it and built it into the design through a multipurpose area, where tables can be fitted together as the need arises. This space can be used not only for small-scale meetings, but also for learning sessions and for all company meetings—and it also serves as a break room. A third thing people told us that they wanted was a Wellness Room, a small room for private time. That might be time people need alone for a short personal break or a private phone call, or for times when nursing mothers need some privacy. We built that into the plan, too.

"Those are the kinds of discussions we like to have, and the kinds of ideas we like to generate. The results were tailored to our team because the communication was tailored to our team. I like to think that our emphasis on communication and consultation is part of the reason we have very little turnover here. We have some very creative people who have been part of the team here at Blue Book for fifty years, and we're quite proud of that."

Surprise, surprise: When you let people share their ideas about how to make their own experience in the workplace better, they feel better about sharing ideas in other areas, as well!

Jim Carr's company offers a great example for companies of all sizes: Look for reasons to start a discussion about the kinds of changes people would like to see in their work spaces! And just in case you were wondering, no, you definitely don't have to wait for a major building redesign to have these kinds of discussions with your team members.

As Great Workplace Revolution Coach, are you looking for new ways to engage with individuals and groups to improve the working environment? Are you asking people, both as they begin to work for your organization and at regular intervals after that, "What do you need from us in order to do a great job?"

Takeaways for the Great Workplace Revolution Coach:

- Use major (or minor!) changes in workplace environment design as opportunities to communicate with your team, to discuss the changes you have in mind, and to collect good design ideas from your people.

- As in the values discussion (see Strategy #1), engage the team as you refine and finalize the design. The final design should be the conclusion of in-depth conversations.

- Emphasize design elements of the workplace that have multiple uses, and look for new ways spaces can be configured to serve multiple purposes. A flexible, adaptive, creative physical workspace is one of the best ways to attract, support, and retain a flexible, adaptive, and creative team.

Great Workplace Revolution Strategy #3: Put the right person in the right job.

KEY CONCEPT: Identify each team member's actual workplace strengths, and encourage people to play to those strengths.

Case Study for Putting the Right Person in the Right Job: Thomas Interior Systems

"I'd rather take my chances on people with good instincts than a genius who can explain why their start-up failed."

— **MARC ANDREESSEN**, co-author of Mosaic and Netscape, the first widely-used web browser

When it comes to recruiting and assigning your team members, I can attest, from personal experience, that "gut instinct" is not enough.

One of the biggest challenges of launching and sustaining a successful Great Workplace Revolution is connecting the right person with the right assignments. If people aren't in the right jobs, if their skills aren't being utilized to the fullest, if their assignments aren't delivering the kind of personal and professional challenge that supports growth and development... then why in the world should a creative person choose to stick around?

At some level, I think, all of us who must make hiring and placement decisions know this, yet there is a problem. We don't always act on what we know. Most of us, at least initially, believe that our own "gut instinct" is enough to ensure the placement of the right person in the right position. In reality, though, that isn't enough.

Regardless of the industry in which you operate, regardless of the size of your organization, and regardless of the current market share that you enjoy, your enterprise will benefit from a formal person-by-person assessment that tells you both the strengths and the potential blind spots of each individual in the organization. And make no mistake, we *all* have strengths and we *all* have blind spots.

One of those blind spots, invariably, is a potentially unhealthy tendency to assume that people whose workplace priorities and aptitudes are similar to our own tend to be right, while others tend to be wrong. This is what managerial gut instinct really boils down to, and whatever we choose to call it, it is a major disincentive for employees whose working style, aptitudes, and insights differ from our own. Yet these people who view the world in ways very different from the way we view it are not wrong. To the contrary, they are essential to our organization's success and to our own success, and we must make every effort to engage them, understand them, and listen to them.

Here's the bottom line: We are, all of us, biased toward our own modus operandi (that is, our customary way of doing things). To overcome this built-in managerial obstacle to launching a Great Workplace Revolution, we need some kind of formal assessment system.

Some formal assessment system is essential for any organization committed to placing the right person in the right job—and this commitment is an essential element of a Great Workplace Revolution.

Assessing Our People

"We must look into other people, as well as at them."
— **PHILIP DORMER STANHOPE**,
4th Earl of Chesterfield (1694–1773),
British statesman and man of letters.

There are dozens of assessment systems out there, some of them more helpful than others. Over the years, I've tested many of them first-hand. I'd like to share some thoughts on the system that we use at our company, and tell you why we have built that assessment system into the DNA of our organization. The hiring and assessment tool we use, after having tested and evaluated many of the major systems on the market (as well as a number of minor ones) is the Kolbe RightFit program, offered by Kolbe Corp. (www.kolbe.com).

Kolbe's system makes identifying the right person for the job, and assigning the right task to the right person, far easier and far less expensive than the gut-instinct method followed by most entrepreneurs and executives with hiring responsibility. Kolbe's tools allow organizations of all sizes to evaluate candidates not merely on their (stated) past experience, but on what ends up mattering far more in the day-to-day reality of the workplace: the natural instincts of each candidate and team member.

I realize that many people reading this will have done their own research on this question of how best to assess employees, and I realize that my emphasis, and Kolbe's emphasis, on "natural instincts" may sound unconventional or even unscientific. What is important to understand, though, is that Kolbe's system delivers better results for us than the various personality-type programs out there... and it does so without relying on personality "types." Instead, it identifies four scientifically verifiable ways of effectively analyzing people, activities, and relationships based on the best current research on human brain function. And that extensive research identifies certain natural, instinctive patterns.

Kolbe's assessment system helps you identify the methods of operation that a team member or candidate actually uses right now, whenever he or she is striving to attain, solve, or create something. All you as the team or organizational leader really need to do is become familiar with the basic modes that relate, not to that individual's personality (whatever that is) but to the verifiable human brain processes he or she uses to get things done.

Kolbe's statistically proven tools identify each individual's levels of intuitive comfort in four critical areas, and assigns a numerical value within each area. This system creates a practical, realistic summary of the individual's strengths and potential challenge areas. Any individual's Kolbe result is so personalized that only 5% of the general population is likely to have one just like it.

Our own experience with the Kolbe system has been that it has dramatically enhanced retention, workplace efficiency, and job satisfaction. And our company is not alone. According to Kolbe, one national financial services company using the system estimates saving more than $10 million from improved interviewing and human resources processes, and from reduced downtime. Another employer reports that 0% of the employees hired using RightFit left for job-related reasons. Yes, you read that right: *zero percent.*

I was fortunate enough to interview Kathy Kolbe, founder of Kolbe Corp. and creator of the RightFit system, the system my company has been using with great success for the past 15 years. Let's take a closer look at the astonishingly accurate assessment system she has developed.

Focusing on Your Strengths—and Everyone Else's

> *"Success is achieved by developing our strengths, not by eliminating our weaknesses."*
> — **MARILYN VOS SAVANT,** American author

The Kolbe system is powered by a simple four-digit summary that can (and, I believe, should) identify the core workplace assets of any individual working for your team or applying to work for it. The summary that gives you this information is known as the Kolbe A™ Index.

"The Index," Kathy Kolbe told me, "is designed to help you focus on your strengths, and thereby get a better understanding of how you do things when you are free to do them your own way. When you're in the zone, in that glide pattern, when you are out of your relaxation mode and into your mode of striving for something, what do you do most and what do you do least? How do you go about making decisions? What is your instinctive, preferred way of approaching a task? The Index answers these questions, and helps you celebrate your strengths by focusing on what you naturally do well."

The Kolbe system does this by assigning numerical one-to-ten rankings in four ACTION MODES that reflect classic human problem-solving tactics. According to Kathy, understanding how we use these four MOs—modes of operation—is essential to building and supporting any team.

"The Index," she explains, "shows everybody on the team that everyone else is somewhere on the continuum in each of these four areas. However you are is just fine for you. There is no good or bad, no right or wrong. Who you are is how you were meant to be.

Understanding where you and others land in the four Action Modes means you are validating and celebrating strengths you can use in decision-making that are always there for you and will always be there for you... recognizing that others have different strengths."

The four action modes that the Kolbe A™ Index measures go by the following labels:

- FACT FINDER
- FOLLOW THROUGH
- QUICK START
- IMPLEMENTOR

Let's look more closely at Kathy Kolbe's descriptions of how these modes of operation work. According to Kolbe, "There is a major difference between the way you function when you are relaxed and at rest and the way you function when you take action. When you take action, when you strive, when you start getting things done in the way that feels most instinctive and natural to you, you do so through a mixture of four different Action Modes, with a strong likelihood of favoring one or two of these modes over the others. These Action Modes are not 'personality types,' but instinct-based MOs that can be expressed using a simple numerical system."

Kolbe's continuum of instinct-based Action Modes breaks down as follows:

- The FACT FINDER Action Mode is all about how people gather and share information. Are they more inclined to simplify a point ... or to specify/explain it?

- The FOLLOW THROUGH Action Mode is all about how people arrange, design, sort, and store information. Are they more inclined to adapt to a set of facts... or to systematize?

- The QUICK START Action Mode is all about how people deal with risk and uncertainty. Are they more inclined to stabilize and play it safe... or to improvise and see what happens?

- The IMPLEMENTOR Action Mode is all about how people handle space and tangibles. Are they more inclined to imagine and theorize, or to build, repair, trouble-shoot, and practice?

There is no right answer to any of these questions. As Kathy Kolbe is quick to point out, each of these instinctive working styles is right for the person who is naturally drawn to it. "Every numerical rating on the Kolbe Continuum," she reminds us, "represents an equally positive trait." My own Kolbe profile, for the record, is Fact Finder 4, Follow Through 6, Quick Start 8, and Implementor 2.

My Kolbe score is not inherently good or bad. It is simply who I am. It is highly unlikely that you and I would bring exactly the same MO, the same highly personalized striving approach, to the workplace. And our shared workplace is going to be all the richer for that! This is perhaps the biggest Kolbe takeaway for anyone who is eager to launch a Great Workplace Revolution: A healthy organization needs a team that can, communally, provide a wide variety of striving styles! So by helping you understand these styles, the Kolbe system helps you not only to get the right people on the bus, but also to make sure the right people are sitting in the right seats on the bus!

Up to this point, I've shared with you why I feel so strongly that a personnel assessment system is essential, how I've reached the conclusion that the Kolbe Continuum is the most accurate tool available, and a little bit about how the Kolbe system evaluates your team members. Now, it's time for me to share my own organization's experiences with the Kolbe system.

I should share one of my critical discoveries in this area. It has to do with figuring out what the Kolbe system is not. It's definitely not an IQ test! Most of us are familiar with the terms "IQ" and "Intelligence Quotient," and we may even have grown up believing that tests of cognitive ability (like IQ tests) reflect how smart an applicant or an employee is, and, by extension, how likely he or she is to help our organization. Yet how many smart people can we think of who were also very bad hires? I can think of quite a few from my own experience. What was going on in these situations? Why did hiring a smart person not result in a good fit?

The answer lies in understanding that the human mind is three-dimensional, and *cognitive* (that is, logical) ability is just one of those dimensions. Getting someone to interact effectively with other three-dimensional human minds to work toward organizational goals requires a clearer understanding of the other two dimensions. According to Kolbe. those are *affect* (also known as emotion) and the little-understood, little-discussed, but vitally important dimension of *conation.*

That's what the four elements of the Kolbe Continuum measure: conation, our instinctive style of approaching a task when we are left to our own devices. Each of the instinctive action styles is a conative strength. If we don't have a clear sense of how a given individual's conative strengths line up with his or her responsibilities, or with the conative strengths of the other people he or she will be working with, we are likely to find ourselves with the wrong people on the bus... or with the right people burning out needlessly, because we have placed them in the wrong seats on the bus!

Are Your People in the Right Seat on the Bus?

"At the end of the day you bet on people, not on strategies."
— **LARRY BOSSIDY,** former CEO, AlliedSignal

It's time to share a true story that serves as an example of how important an understanding of conation really is for the Great Workplace Revolution Coach. This story will, I hope, illustrate what I mean when I talk about the high price of not getting the right people on the bus, or of putting the right people in the wrong seats on the bus.

A year or so before I assessed my own Kolbe profile (which I believe is an essential first step for anyone who plans on implementing the system in this book), I hired an administrative assistant whom I'll call Pam. I honestly thought I had made a good hire. The truth is, however, that I was flying blind.

Was Pam smart? She certainly was. Did she and I have a good working relationship? Absolutely. Did she and I respect each other and understand what each was trying to do? No doubt about it. Did we each have the best of intentions? Of course we did. And yet something wasn't quite right. Although Pam was very good at running interference for me by keeping others away when I needed free time to work on projects, that just wasn't enough to make this working relationship pan out.

Tasks that I delegated to Pam kept falling through the cracks. Calls that had come in for me went unlogged, unmentioned, and unreturned. Questions I had asked her to explore went unaddressed. Important customers who had asked me (through Pam) to take care of essential questions got frustrated when they saw no action from my office, and went to the competition.

After I had my own Kolbe profile done, and compared it to Pam's, I immediately saw the problem. Pam and I were just too similar. In fact, our profiles were almost identical. Her Quick Start numbers were notably high, just as mine are. That meant that, like me, she was essentially an improviser. I didn't need another improviser. I needed an implementor! Her Implementor numbers, however, were low, just like mine. She was just as likely to overlook, oversimplify, and underestimate the importance of critical details as I was. The truth was, I had made a poor recruiting choice. I hadn't hired someone who could compensate for my blind spots. I had hired someone who amplified them!

This wasn't Pam's mistake. It was mine. I had fallen prey to the Halo Effect, a classic hiring error. I had seen a few traits that reminded me of an employee whom I liked, admired, and wanted to see more of (namely, myself!). I had made my hiring decision based on those similarities, not on the true requirements of the job or the interpersonal requirements of the team. Because of that hiring mistake, I had needlessly made life a lot more difficult for myself, my organization, and ultimately for Pam. We parted amicably.

I now know that the ideal assistant for me is not someone with a mirror-image profile, but someone whose strengths compensate for my weak areas. We all have strengths and weak areas. The only real question is, is the team we're on right now deploying our strengths to maximum advantage, and compensating for the areas where we need support? Or has it put us in the wrong seat on the bus?

Are You Flying Blind?

"There is a condition worse than physical blindness, and that is, seeing something that isn't there."

— **THOMAS HARDY** (1840–1928),
English novelist and poet-

One of the most common mistakes executives and entrepreneurs are likely to make is assuming that someone who has a given skill is, by definition, going to be good at leading a team that needs to master and implement that skill. A truly effective personal assessment system, such as the Kolbe Index, makes that kind of mistake much less likely. On the other hand, if you do not have that kind of system in place, you will be flying blind.

Here is one classic scenario: Stan Superstar had exceeded his quota for the last five straight quarters. He was clearly the ace of the sales staff. Last week, Stan's manager for the last five years suddenly took a job offer at an overseas company, which left Ernie Entrepreneur, founder and president of the Acme Company, facing a challenge: How to keep the sales staff humming, avoid a long period of "leadership vacuum" listlessness while the search for a new VP of sales unfolded, and keep Stan engaged and challenged? For Ernie, the decision practically made itself. Make Stan the new VP of Sales! He had lunch with Stan, asked whether he was up for the challenge, got an enthusiastic yes, and announced his decision to the rest of the company just two days after the old VP of sales's departure.

Both Stan and Ernie were flying blind, and both were headed

for disaster. Had Ernie (the prime mover in the promotion) used the Kolbe system, he would have known that the extremely successful departing VP of sales had high Kolbe scores in the Follow Through and Fact Finder modes, which meant he excelled at spotting patterns, creating processes that others could use, and documenting which tactics actually worked (and which didn't) in the real-world situations that the sales team faced every day.

Stan, on the other hand, would have posted extremely low scores in Follow Through and Fact Finder if he had been evaluated using the Kolbe system, and he would have shown extremely high scores in the Quick Start mode. That's a classic profile for an effective salesperson, and one that countless successful entrepreneurs, including Ernie, shared. People like Stan and Ernie are instinctively talented when it comes to spotting opportunities, establishing emotional connections with likely prospects, and generating excitement about beginning a new relationship or continuing one. It sometimes seems to outsiders that such people are "born to sell." What Stan and Ernie were not born to do, however, was create documents, policies, learning initiatives, and coaching programs capable of supporting people less talented than themselves.

None of this was obvious, however, at the time Ernie announced his decision to the rest of the company. As he gathered the team and shared the news of Stan's promotion, he actually thought he was solving three problems at once. First and foremost (in Ernie's view), he was preventing a leadership vacuum in the critical period following the unexpected departure of his previous sales manager. Second, he was proving to his staff that he was committed to the principle of promoting from within. Third, he was hiring someone he felt he could trust. He had a gut feeling about this.

That is what Ernie assumed he was doing by promoting Stan. As it turned out, though, two of those three assumptions were totally misguided, and the third was only partially correct.

Ernie *was not* preventing a leadership vacuum. He was creating one. Stan struggled in his new role, and the department's revenue took a sharp nosedive, as did morale among the members of the sales staff.

Ernie *did not* send the message to his staff that he was committed to promoting from within. After three months, he had to fire Stan, because Stan (a competitive player with a strong sense that he deserved the spotlight) refused to return to his old selling position. To do so would have been to admit defeat, and that was something Stan wasn't good at. The "divorce" was an ugly one.

Finally, Ernie's gut feeling that he could trust Stan in everything turned out to be way off base. What Ernie's gut was actually telling him was that he and Stan had a great deal in common—which was certainly true. When the relationship turned sour, however, Stan turned out to be more than willing to say terrible things about Ernie and his company to anyone and everyone who would listen. That long list of people included every member of Ernie's sales staff!

Ernie's long, sad, and (unfortunately) quite common story is one that could have been prevented quite easily with a realistic assessment of each character's instinctive modes of operation!

As Great Workplace Revolution Coach, are you clear on your own conative strengths? Can you accurately identify the conative strengths of others? Can you help your organization assemble a diverse team that draws on multiple, complementary conative strengths?

Takeaways for the Great Workplace Revolution Coach:

- Visit Kolbe.com and get yourself assessed .... so that you can identify and capitalize on your own conative strengths.
- Then, get your team assessed ... so that you can identify and help them capitalize on their conative strengths.

- Advocate for the use of the Kolbe assessment system **at all levels of your organization.**

Great Workplace Revolution Strategy #4: Provide constant accommodation to, and understanding of, the whole employee.

KEY CONCEPT: No matter how much or how little money you have to spend, your team members can sense whether you are supporting them or are apathetic towards them as fellow human beings.

Case Study for Understanding and Accommodating the Whole Employee: Southwest Airlines

"I don't care how poor a man is, if he has family, he's rich."

— **DAN WILCOX** and **THAD MUMFORD**,
American television writing team

"The strength of the team is each individual member. The strength of each member is the team."

— **PHIL JACKSON**,
retired American basketball player and coach

To launch a Great Workplace Revolution, management must understand, care for, and support each employee as a complete individual. This requires both a conscious, carefully considered plan for engaging each member of the team, and a willingness to engage in spontaneous discussions with individuals based on their unique experiences, aspirations, and needs. It is a lot of work.

We are talking now about the neglected art of making the workplace a zone for ongoing acceptance and support. We are talking about treating the individual as an individual, not merely as someone who shows up, contributes, leaves at the end of the day, and draws a paycheck every two weeks. In a very real sense, we are talking about making the workplace environment an extension of a team member's family environment. If you're a front-line manager, that means (to begin with) knowing the names of a few of the family members of each and every person who reports to you.

That is a test that most team leaders would not pass. Yet supporting the whole employee means a great deal more than this. It means building a weekly work schedule that leaves the employee ample time for family commitments. It means knowing what major transitional events (births, illnesses, departures to college, care for aging parents, and so on) are happening within the employee's family circle, and what transitional events are on the horizon. It means finding a way to welcome the employee's family in the workplace. It means creating a level of personal trust and collaboration with employees that inspires them to come to us when something important happens in their home life, so that we can work collaboratively to craft a solution that makes sense for everyone. At the end of the day, supporting the whole employee means the person's direct supervisor is paying enough attention and listening well enough, not just once in a while but consistently, to make sure the employee never, ever feels that he or she must choose between work and family. Work life and home life must be completely complementary parts of a single whole, and if they're not, then the team leader must engage directly with the employee until they *are* parts of a single whole.

One of my favorite examples in this area is Southwest Airlines, which is widely regarded as one of the very best companies to work for in America. It offers a jaw-dropping list of employee benefits, including an innovative flex-time policy and free flights for employees. Southwest has been cited so often for its positive workplace culture and supportive work environment that, after a while, the company's long list of accomplishments and awards begins to sound a little like a broken record. At the end of the day, however, it is Southwest's practical employee-first business philosophy that has allowed it to become one of the most sought-after work environments in the country, if not the world.

"You put your employees first and if you take care of them, then they will take good care of you," says Herb Kelleher, the airline's legendary chairman. "Then your customers will come back, and your shareholders will like that, so it's really a unity."

Now, we can write something like that down in a mission statement or a policy manual without much difficulty. The question is, how can we follow through on it in a way that translates into both marketplace success and employee loyalty, as Southwest has done for decades? The airline has turned a profit every year since 1973; its corporate leadership team currently receives a 93% favorable rating from employees, according to Glassdoor.com.

This is one of those areas where management talk is cheap, but where management action can truly make a powerful competitive difference. The kind of understanding I am talking about only comes in a workplace like Southwest's, where management proves its willingness to accommodate real-world employee needs, such as the need for flexible scheduling, through action. If an unexpected shift change has to happen because of a sudden emergency at home, the change in scheduling happens. If employees need support in the areas of flex time, child care, and/or family leave, the employer must make a convincing effort to make that kind of support happen. We must be seen, not to be doing the minimum that the law requires to support our employees, but to be making an honest effort to do the most we possibly can, given the company's resources.

The notion of actually making an effort is key. Whenever people stop making an effort for each other, the relationship suffers. Making an honest effort is what employees expect from the people who are closest to them—spouses, children, and other family members—and it's what they should expect from us as the employer, too.

Low Budget, High Intentionality

> *"You seldom improve quality by cutting costs, but you can often cut costs by improving quality."*
> — **Karl Albrecht**

The quality of our intention as leaders makes all the difference in executing the fourth Great Workplace Revolution strategy, far more difference than our ability to allocate money. Contrary to popular belief, proving that our organization values and supports the whole employee is *not* necessarily a matter of laying out more cash! Depending on your organization's circumstances and its stage of development, you may end up allocating more financial resources to support the members of your team as you launch your Great Workplace Revolution; on the other hand, you may not. The money isn't what matters most. Proving that you support and value each individual employee is what really matters. This is always a matter of refining, clarifying, and improving your organizational intentionality toward a specific individual employee.

To put it another way: You may sometimes have to work with a low budget, but you can always have a high intentionality.

For example: In a perfect world, with a perfect budget, you might want to be able to offer each member of your team a company-paid daycare center with state-of-the-art facilities and a trained, qualified, 100% company-subsidized childcare staff. In the world you actually occupy, you might not be able to offer that just yet. You can, however, spend a couple of afternoons researching locally available daycare options for your team, all the state and local grants and other financial support that may be available, and the very best online resources for local working parents. You can then put all of your research into an easy-to-read handbook, and you can make a page-by-page review of that handbook part of your "onboarding" process with each new employee who has children.

Believe it: The nature of the one-on-one attention you as a leader can devote to issues like childcare—or bereavement, or divorce, or care for aging parents, or any of a dozen other lifestyle and family realities—is, at the end of the day, far more important than the total number of dollars you allocate to these issues. This claim may at first seem farfetched, especially if you are used to working in an organization where the size of the budget is a symbol of a department's importance. All the same, I can promise you that what I am sharing with you here is true.

I have worked with many companies and executives whose resources and benefit packages were ample, but who failed to connect with or engage their team members for the simple reason that they did not prove personal concern, care, and regard for each employee as an individual. "Faking it" simply doesn't work when it comes to employee engagement. On the other hand, what I am advocating here—compassionate intentionality on behalf of your team members—really does work. I believe that the reason it works is quite simple: Caring for others at a one-on-one level is truly the heart and soul of any Great Place To Work.

No Viable Alternative to Caring

> *"Caring about others, running the risk of feeling, and leaving an impact on people, brings happiness."*
>
> — HAROLD KUSHNER, prominent American rabbi

If you stop to consider this question carefully, you'll realize that there actually is no viable alternative to complete, authentic, engaged intentionality with each one of your direct reports. Think about what happens if you let this critical value slip, even for a single exchange, even with only one of your team members. Jack, your top sales performer and one of the most committed employees in the company, walks into your office one day and says, "Boss, I'm going to need to take some time off to deal with some issues at home. I think the next couple of days are going to have to come out of my stock of vacation days. I'm sorry for the short notice, but I really don't have any alternative. I'll do everything I can for you from home, but I need to be able to be away from the office the rest of this week."

As a manager, there are two paths you can walk down in this situation. The first path, the one I'm advocating here, is to instantly send Jack the message that you trust him, that you understand that these kinds of things come up from time to time, and that, together, you will find a way to make the arrangement he is suggesting work. If the relationship permits, and only if it permits, you might ask Jack to let you know something about what's going on at home, not so you can judge whether or not this is really something worth giving Jack some flexibility in scheduling over the next couple of days, but to find out how you can support Jack better.

But what happens if you don't follow that path?

What happens if you get distracted by the fact that Jack is working on a big deal with a potential major account that's ready to close this week? What if you start doubting whether Jack can fulfill all his responsibilities *and* take care of whatever personal problem he has to deal with? What if you start thinking about the "bottom line" first and the people second?

In that case, you might be tempted to say (as many before you have said), "Jack, I completely sympathize with whatever problem you may be running into at home, but if you check your employee handbook and your job description, you'll see that they both state quite clearly that working hours need to be spent either in the field with customers and prospects, or here at the office. What's more, vacation days need to be scheduled at a time that's mutually convenient for management and employees, and those days need to be set up at least three weeks in advance. I'll see you in here tomorrow morning bright and early at eight a.m. as usual. Thanks for understanding, Jack."

Or, if you're a real coward, you could say, "Let me see what I can do," and then send Jack a terse e-mail after-hours apologizing to Jack for your inability to set up this time off for him.

Let me tell you what's going to happen if you say either of those things to Jack, or any variation on them. First, Jack is going to take the time at home that he needs, regardless of what you say. He may tell you that he's gotten sick, he may tell you that he's out visiting a client, he may tell you that he's stuck in traffic court, but he's going to do what he needs to do, and it's not going to bother him that he's lying to you, because he no longer trusts you. Why should he?

Not only that—Jack is going to start looking for work elsewhere. You're going to lose one of your best and brightest, probably to a direct competitor. And if you imagine that that's the worst consequence of reciting the "letter of the law" to Jack, think again. Between that day and the day he leaves your company—whether it's a week later or several (less productive) years later—he will be talking to other employees about your little speech, and he won't be saying nice things about it.

What Jack says at the water cooler while you're not around could sound like this:

> "Do you know what he/she said when I asked for time off to visit my mom while she was dying in the hospital? He told me to read my job description and file all my requests for time off three weeks in advance!"

Did Jack tell you his mom was sick? No. He shouldn't have to.

Did he tell you she was terminally ill and in the hospital? No. He shouldn't have to do that, either.

Is it fair that he lumps those undisclosed facts into the story whenever he passes it along to others, so that it makes you look like the bad guy? Yes! It's completely fair, because you made a classic management mistake. You chose to focus on (short-term) economic interests before (long-term) people interests. You forgot that it is *people* who make positive bottom line performance possible in the first place. As a result, you not only lost Jack (and all the deals he would have closed if he had stayed on longer with your organization and worked at full capacity), but you also lost the good will of everyone with whom he shared his water-cooler story!

What do you do about employees who abuse your trust? Does supporting the whole employee mean seeing people through problems like substance abuse or anger management? We'll look at these important questions next.

"Problem" Cases: The Leadership Challenge

> *"Leadership is a combination of strategy and character. If you must be without one, be without the strategy."*
> — GEN. H. NORMAN SCHWARZKOPF

> *"If your actions inspire others to dream more, learn more, do more, and become more, you are a leader."*
> — Anonymous

I run into a lot of people who ask me, "What about those employees who game the system? What about the ones we suspect of calling in sick when they're not sick? What about the ones we have a gut feeling about, a feeling that they just can't be trusted to tell you the truth about why they need time off or support? Are we supposed to give them wholehearted support, too?"

Yes. We're supposed to start by assuming the best. Why? Because it's what we want our employees to do when they're interacting with customers (or anyone else). To assume otherwise is to lose sight of the Golden Rule—DO UNTO OTHERS AS YOU WOULD HAVE THEM DO UNTO YOU. This is a time-tested managerial principle if ever there was one, and a moral compass that I for one would like to be able hold on to as a manager, an executive, and a leader.

I realize, of course, that not everyone reading this book will share my faith in the Golden Rule, and will be searching this text for something more pragmatic. That's fine. Here's a pragmatic response to this classic managerial dilemma: "Would you rather have a problem with one employee who abuses your trust, whom everyone else on your team tries to correct, or a problem with an entire team where everyone is coordinating their efforts to abuse your trust and keep you in the dark?"

That, unfortunately, is the choice we face as leaders. Look first at what I call Option One, the first and best option: If we present authentic intentionality, if we ask with genuine interest about what's happening in the person's life and to the person's loved ones, if we make it clear that we really are eager to work together to address personal issues constructively when they arise, then we send the right message to our team as a whole, and run the risk that, every once in a while, someone will attempt to take advantage of us. If that happens, however, it happens in a environment where other employees are likely to volunteer to be our "eyes and ears," and where our team members reinforce the behavior we're trying to encourage, and criticize the behavior we're trying to eliminate. Caring about the employee as a person is the first, and best, option if you intend to launch a successful Great Workplace Revolution.

Of course, there's always Option Two: Treat your employees like perpetually errant schoolchildren whom you don't trust enough to make independent choices. If you do that consistently enough, they will place you in the same mental compartment where they've stored all their memories of their least favorite teacher from school. In that case, you'll be virtually guaranteeing that not one, but a working majority (at least) of your employees will talk behind your back, form cliques that see management as the personal embodiment of all that is Wrong With the World, and find interesting ways to keep you from figuring out what's really happening at any given moment.

It's actually a pretty straightforward choice when you stop to think about it. In fact, it's a choice that virtually makes itself. Choose Option One!

None of this is meant to suggest that you must give a free pass to an employee who proves that he or she has no intention of abiding by the basic rules of the road of working for your firm. In the case of employees who show, over time, a clear pattern of violating your company's core values (see Strategy One), you have an equally clear duty to part company, and sooner rather than later. Making it easier to part company with such people, by the way, is one of the two big reasons you identify core values in the first place: These are the traits for which you will both hire *and* fire. However, we need to be brutally honest with ourselves as leaders. If we keep having to deal with employees who make a sustained effort to violate our company's core values, there is something wrong with our hiring system, our performance evaluation system, our retention system, or some combination of the three! By the way: If these systems *are* working properly, most of your actual "problem employees" will decide on their own that it is time to leave your organization, because it will be obvious to them that they are no longer operating in harmony with the values they were hired for in the first place.

In the extremely difficult situation where someone who once supported and upheld your company's core values, but is now unable to do so as the result of a substance abuse problem, there are no easy answers, beyond the obvious one that such decisions should be approached on a case-by-case basis, and should be made, whenever possible, with the help and guidance of the organization's senior management. In our case, I can only share the fact that we have had to deal with this situation in our company's history twice, and that we tried, on both occasions, to give the employee the physical, medical, and emotional support necessary to turn the situation around. In one case, we were able to save the relationship (and the employee); in the other, we were not. The only certainty here, I am afraid, is that failing to intervene through getting professional help, is likely to leave both the company and the employee far worse off.

As Great Workplace Revolution Coach, are you genuinely interested in what is happening in each employee's life outside of the workplace? Do you make a strong personal effort to support your team members (with options like flex time and additional time off) if they need that support to address problems at home? Do you show high intentionality, even when you are working with a low budget?

Takeaways for the Great Workplace Revolution Coach:

- Make sure supervisors know (at least) the first names of each of their direct reports' close family members. Start this trend by learning about your own direct reports' families!

- Be supportive when challenges arise in an employee's home life. Give employees the benefit of the doubt when deciding when and how to offer support.

- Show high person-to-person intentionality... regardless of the size of your budget.

Great Workplace Revolution Strategy #5: Build into the culture appropriate recognition for a job well done.

KEY CONCEPT: A workplace without appropriate recognition is a workplace without loyalty.

"When someone comes along who genuinely thanks us, we will follow that person a very long way."

— **ALAN LOY MCGINNIS** (1933–2005), American author and psychotherapist

"Appreciation is a powerful tool to shift perspective. Finding something to appreciate during a difficult situation quickly moves the perspective to the big picture from the little picture."

— **DOC CHILDRE** and **BRUCE CRYER**, Co-authors of *From Chaos to Coherence (The Power to Change Performance)*

"A pat on the back is only a few vertebrae removed from a kick in the pants... but is miles ahead in results."

— **ELLA WHEELER WILCOX** (1850–1919), American poet

If you were to ask any one hundred leaders to tell you how important it is to offer employees some kind of appropriate recognition and reinforcement when they do something right, I believe the odds are good that ninety-five of them would say that such recognition is extremely important to the success of their enterprise. And yet, most employees feel, and rightly so, that recognition for a job well done is a scarce commodity indeed in their own workplace.

As leaders, most of us already know how important it is for us to offer our people positive reinforcement for doing the right thing. We may even put up posters or signs offering generic praise for the team as a whole, and tell our direct reports about the importance of acknowledging specific achievements in the workplace. What we may not be so sure about is how to make recognition for the individual member of the team a daily workplace reality.

Recognition for a job well done is one of those things that leaders talk about a great deal, but only rarely manage to build into the organizational DNA. I say this not to denigrate anyone, but merely to call attention to the fact that leaders face a great many problems on the average day. Catching the people we work with in the act of doing something right does not always naturally rise to the top of our to-do list.

The truth is, actually executing on this Great Workplace Revolution Strategy takes a great deal of sustained effort. It means looking beyond the crisis of the moment. It means developing a special kind of patience, the kind of patience that combines pragmatism and problem-solving with the ability to disengage from issues that seem larger than they actually are and find the silver lining for both the individual and the team. This takes practice, and it is hard to do on a regular basis even when we know we are supposed to do it, have a firm personal intention to do it, and tell those around us that we know we have a duty to do it. We're human beings. We have a lot of responsibilities, we face a lot of challenges, and we will sometimes lose perspective.

All of which means that, when it comes to weaving appropriate recognition for a job well done into the DNA of our organization, we shouldn't expect our best intentions to do the job for us. We need a system.

Why Bother with a System?

> *"If you can't describe what you are doing as a process*
> *then you don't know what you're doing."*
>
> — **W. Edwards Deming** (1900–1993),
> American statistician, professor, author

I believe that, in any enterprise where there is a system in place that delivers authentic, meaningful, reality-based personal recognition, and where the organization's guiding values are both positive and clear, anything is possible. At such organizations, the ritual of passing along appreciation for a job well done becomes part of What It Means To Work Here. That kind of habit, that kind of ritual, that kind of system, when combined with a genuine sense of mission, can overcome even major deficits in many of the other areas we are examining in this book. And, just as significant for Great Workplace Revolution Coaches operating in entrepreneurial and startup environments, it can help overcome deficits in financial compensation.

Just as it was with the "getting the right person in the right bus, and in the right *seat* in the bus" strategy, creating a workable, repeatable system for appropriate recognition should be a non-negotiable priority for the Great Workplace Revolution Coach. Consider the following:

Recently, a national survey of 350 human-resources professionals found that "the greatest factor in workplace productivity is a positive environment in which employees feel appreciated."

According to a 2003 Gallup study, 61% of American workers "received no praise" in the workplace. Not "a little" praise. Not "infrequent" praise. *No* praise! The same study found that the single biggest reason most people leave their jobs is a feeling of not being appreciated.

On the other hand, the Gallup research has also shown that workers who *do* receive regular praise and acknowledgement for their accomplishments have higher rates of productivity, receive higher satisfaction scores from the customers with whom they interact, are more engaged with other employees, have fewer accidents on the job, and (last but not least) are less likely to quit their jobs.

Is wide scale disengagement and disaffection—which is what 61% of our workers are reporting—an obstacle to a Great Workplace Revolution? Absolutely. Is avoiding that kind of disengagement and disaffection worth some time and effort? It is. Benefits like the ones identified in the Gallup survey, and countless other surveys, give us a clear reason for establishing a system that ensures ongoing, authentic, reality-based recognition in the workplace. This is not a "nice-to-have" element of the Great Workplace Revolution. This is a "must-have"!

A Word of Caution about "Public Praise"

> *"Feeling appreciated is one of the most important needs that people have. When you share with someone your appreciation and gratitude, they will not forget you. Appreciation will return to you many times."*
> — **STEVE BRUNKHORST**, life strategies coach

> *"Recognition is the greatest motivator."*
> — **GERARD C. EAKEDALE**

You may have noticed that this Great Workplaces Revolution strategy emphasizes recognition for a job well done, rather than public praise or public recognition. There's a very important reason for this, and I want to be sure it lands as a best practice for anyone who is building the kind of system we're talking about creating here.

Most employees will respond favorably, and perhaps even passionately, to the prospect of being praised in front of their peers for a job well done. For this majority of the workforce, tactics like singling out the employee during a team meeting, or naming him or her as Employee of the Month, or asking the team member to share ideas during the "morning huddle," can have a powerful, direct, dramatic, and long-lasting effect on engagement and morale. For these employees, bestowing attention, applause, and praise in front of their peers is one of the most effective (and cost-effective!) managerial tools for employee engagement in both the short and long terms.

Yet it is just as important for the Great Workplace Revolution Coach to understand that public praise almost certainly is *not* an effective motivator for everyone on your team.

For some employees, being singled out for *anything* in public, whether positive or negative, is a personal nightmare that they will do just about anything to avoid—up to and including leaving your organization. Some people, and probably a minority of the people on your team, are just not "wired" to respond positively to the experience of being in the spotlight. In fact, they will only call attention to themselves when there is absolutely no alternative, and are very likely to feel traumatized afterward. That means you will have to customize your approach, and learn, through informal personal interviews, who on your staff will welcome all that attention... and who would just as soon receive a quieter, less attention-drawing form of recognition, such as a gift card to a favorite store or a paid day off.

Recall that the guiding principle behind this Great Workplace Revolution strategy, and indeed behind all twelve of the strategies, is *tailoring*. That means customization. It means one-on-one communication. It means learning what works and what doesn't for one employee at a time, and then using what you've learned to create an environment in which that employee feels safe, respected, and listened to.

With all that in mind, let's look at an organization that has implemented a world-class, customized, and flexible employee recognition program, in service of a successful Great Workplaces Revolution.

Case Study for Appropriate Employee Recognition: Building Services, Inc.

Ralph Kuehn, CEO of Building Services, Inc., based in Milwaukee, Wisconsin, shares some thoughts on offering employees the kind of appropriate recognition that builds long-term loyalty.

"Years ago, I started a habit of sending an end-of-year thank-you letter to the spouse of each and every associate, personally signed by the president of the company—me. Let's say the employee was a married man. I might thank his wife for all the sacrifices she made by letting her husband work odd hours... or apologize for the fact that he had had to miss a family event to take care of a customer. I would acknowledge all the time spent out on the road and all the time away from home, for the hard work her husband had done over the past year, and I would include plenty of details that proved it wasn't just a form letter. I'd describe the husband's typical work day. Then I would send the letter off to the family's home, addressed to the wife! And of course, if it was a female employee, I'd address it to the husband. If the person was unmarried, I'd send it to him or her personally.

"What an impact those letters had! The spouse would read it out loud, the kids would hear it, and of course the associate felt ten feet tall. The husband or wife would say things like, 'I had no idea you were that important over there.' That's one of the ways we were able to hold on to good people.

"There's a variation on that letter that has become very popular now at our company. When someone goes above and beyond the call, we don't wait until the end of the year. We write the family right away. Just last weekend, we had an emergency come up on a project, and in order to keep the customer happy, we had to ask twelve people to come in on a Saturday. They did a great job, and the customer's problem was completely resolved. A few days later, the family of each one of those associates got a letter thanking them personally for making the sacrifice when their loved one came in on Saturday to keep our customer happy. Each letter was signed by the owners of the firm, and contained a gift certificate for the family! You think that kind of personal appreciation has an impact? Absolutely! The spouse and the whole family—maybe even the mother-in-law—step back and say, 'WOW! What a great place to work!' That's the kind of thing that makes your organization stand out from the crowd. That's the kind of attention that builds loyalty—not just in the employee, but in the family."

Notice that Ralph's end-of-year letter is a system—a repeatable process that leaders can understand, implement, and reinforce over time. Once you have a basic system like that in place, whether it is based on some kind of timed message or on specific events that trigger some kind of recognition, you can then introduce refinements and variations on that system, such as the above-and-beyond-the-call letter described above.

Takeaways for the Great Workplace Revolution Coach:

- Create a system for recognition of individual employee achievements and accomplishments.

- Build this system around timed messages (for instance, every three months, every six months, or every year, based on what you feel is right for your organization) or around the attainment of specific performance targets (such as closing a sale of a certain size or receiving high marks for customer satisfaction).

- As you design, test, and implement your system, bear in mind that even though most people enjoy public praise and recognition, some people don't. Make sure there are alternative forms of recognition for team members who would prefer to have their accomplishments acknowledged privately.

Great Workplace Revolution Strategy #6: Support a truly collaborative workplace, both physically and emotionally.

KEY CONCEPT: Your workplace must encourage people to connect, not cut them off from one another.

> *"If two men on the same job agree all the time, then one is useless. If they disagree all the time, both are useless."*
>
> — **DARRYL F. ZANUCK** (1902–1979), American producer, writer, actor, director, and studio executive

Collaborative Workplace... or Cubicle?

Here's an interesting experiment. Ask a creative person who has a job, but who doesn't work for you, to describe his or her physical workspace. Ask, "How would you describe the space where you work?" I will bet you a nickel that you hear one or both of these words in response:

- Office
- Cubicle

Now, another interesting experiment. Count the number of times you hear that creative person use the words "just" or "only." As in:

"It's really *just* an office. Pretty much like any other office."

Or:

"I've *only* got a cubicle. It's not really anything fancy."

What can we learn from these two experiments?

First, we can learn that there are a whole lot of creative people out there who see themselves as more or less trapped in their jobs, stuck within physical workspaces that cut them off from other people. Don't the words "office" and "cubicle" sound like traps to you? I don't know about you, but "office" and "cubicle" really don't describe first places I would choose to spend most of my waking hours if I were given my own way.

Think about this for a moment. There is a reason that a hit workplace TV comedy about an incompetent middle manager is called *The Office.* Most of us associate the word "office" with ineptitude and alienation. The same basic associations apply to "cubicle." These are not the words you would use to convince your relatives, sitting around the Thanksgiving table, that you'd made the right career choice: "Guess what? I get to spend all day in a cubicle! It's part of a larger office, with a lot of other people who are working in cubicles."

Second, we can learn that the creative people themselves know deep down that they could be working in a better environment. Why else would they use words like "just" and "only"?

Now, here's the big question. If you wanted to get one of those creative people to leave his or her current position, and come work for you, how would you describe the physical space? Would you tell the person that she gets to work all day in an office, or spend most of her time in a cubicle? I wouldn't. I'd look for a way to promise her a workspace that enables her to interact with other creative people. So that instead of getting up to go to "just a cubicle" or "only an office" every morning, she could look forward to walking into...

- A brainstorming room.
- A launch center.
- A pitch room.
- A senior creative team center.
- A team space.
- A learning center.
- A creative work environment.
- A collaborative workplace.
- A great workplace.

These kinds of spaces, by their very names, help us make a promise to the employee that special activities take place here: collaboration, engagement, and innovation. These kinds of spaces can inspire people to achieve truly great things... if we keep our promise. That means the spaces must be designed, crafted, and updated with abiding, enduring care.

It is the business of the Great Workplace Revolution Coach to ask great questions about these workspaces. What should they look and feel like? As an organization, how can we create a workspace that speaks of promise, not confinement, to a creative person? Just as important, how can we follow through on that promise?

Designing the Collaborative Workspace

At this point, you may be wondering: What *is* a collaborative workspace?

I believe that it is the responsibility of the leader of any work group to pose that question to each member of the team... to work one-on-one with that person to answer the question uniquely and creatively for each team member, balancing the inclinations and preferences of the individual and the resources available from the organization, and to make good faith efforts to implement that solution in the person's actual working environment. That kind of customization may seem like a daunting task, and I suppose that in the beginning it is. Yet the truth is that the collaborative workspace is different for every individual, and the costs we face as a result of failing to address all the performance, productivity, retention, and morale problems that arise from a "one-size-(supposedly)-fits-all" workplace are far greater.

The trouble is, we've grown used to *those* daily problems. We think of a cramped, anonymous, unfriendly, untailored working area as normal, a part of the everyday experience. We have grown used to low levels of creativity and high turnover rates. Yet, if we were to take the time to learn how each individual defines "collaborative," we would learn that those problems really don't have to be part of the organization's, or the individual's, experience.

Before we get to the critical issue of what we have to do to create a truly collaborative workspace, we should probably get a clear understanding of what we *don't* want to do. Let me share a true story that illustrates one classic mistake that some businesses make. Think of what follows as an anti-case study. (I've changed the details out of respect for the people involved.)

Sharon was an experienced field salesperson who, in her current job, felt like the proverbial square peg in a round hole. She had been working at Company X for two years; she made quota, but never felt she was performing up to her own ability or expectations, despite her long record of success. Why not? Because she was consistently stressed and unhappy at work.

Sharon's supervisor, Ted, had mandated certain amounts of "office time" for all field sales reps, and whenever she was in the office, Sharon was supposed to spend her time in a "boiler room" style sales area that featured a bench-and-table arrangement that she shared with all the other field sales representatives. Ted wanted everyone working together swapping leads, sharing ideas, and plotting next-step strategies. All of this was supposed to unfold in the environment he called the War Room. As a result, Sharon had no private work space, and that was a problem for her.

It's worth noting here that, by situating every member of his team in the War Room, Ted believed he was doing the right thing for the team. It's also worth noting that he believed this for a reason. Ted had gone above and beyond what most executives do. He had actually done research into some of the critical demographic issues that I've shared with you in this book. After completing just a little of that research, Ted quickly realized that most of the people on his team were Millennials who desired a free-flowing, high-energy, face-to-face working environment when they weren't out selling in the field.

In fact, *everyone* on Ted's sales team fit that description—except Sharon.

Sharon was a Baby Boomer who had started her career in a private workspace. What's more, she had scored her biggest sales victories while having regular access to a private work space. (That was at her previous employer.) She wanted that kind of workspace again, but it seemed that the only way she could get it was by working at home, which was something Ted strongly opposed.

The shared space was supposed to encourage a team mentality and a group identity among the members of the sales team, but to Sharon, it felt more like a demotion and an invasion of privacy. The War Room arrangement reminded her of gym class in junior high school, something she had always loathed. She had asked her supervisor to make some changes in her office time, but had only gotten put-offs and lectures about teamwork and personal initiative in return. Ted's message was clear, even though he never actually put it into words: What worked for most of the team would need to work for everyone, including Sharon.

I tell this story because I want to emphasize how easy it is for us to convince ourselves that we have created a collaborative workspace when, in fact, we haven't. Ted, a Traditionalist, knew that he had to make some kind of accommodation to the Millennials on his team, but he was not yet ready to accept the deeper responsibility of a modern leader: Tailoring the workspace to each individual team member. Unless you are willing to do that, you have not yet launched a Great Workplace Revolution!

Facing the prospect of continued stress and alienation from her job, Sharon started a quiet job search and got an interview request from another company. The interview with the CEO let her know that right away that she was looking at a completely different working environment. After hearing her description of the "classroom" work environment where Sharon was spending between fifteen and twenty hours a week, the CEO asked, "What kind of office environment are you looking for?"

Some job interview questions are tough to answer, but Sharon had no trouble at all tackling that one. What was she looking for? What setting did she feel would make her most productive as a professional salesperson? She had been thinking about that for months, years. The answer was simple: a private, glass-walled, literally transparent personal workspace with a door she could shut when she needed privacy. She didn't want to be inaccessible when people required her input or opinions, Sharon explained, and she certainly didn't have any problem attending weekly team meetings. But she did need a door to shut and time to herself.

The CEO said that would be no problem. When could she start?

Sharon took the job in a heartbeat... and never looked back. She quickly became a top salesperson at her new organization, generating over two million dollars a year!

Here are some questions to consider. What would it have cost Ted to have conducted the same kind of conversation with Sharon, and then delivered the same kind of accommodation? About ten minutes of talk time, and perhaps five thousand dollars in remodeling. What did *not* having that conversation cost Ted? Over two million dollars a year in sales revenue, all of which went to a major competitor, and all of which will likely continue to go to that competitor for the balance of Sharon's career.

The moral: One change in the environment, even an intelligent change, does not a collaborative workspace make.

Please understand me correctly. I don't mean to suggest that the workspace Sharon's supervisor designed was inherently wrong. It was a good start. But no workplace can become right until each individual member of the team buys into the plan. Because Ted had a key player—a major revenue producer—who felt uncomfortable with the team-workspace theme, he did not yet have a truly collaborative workspace. He could have created one, if he had wanted to, simply by allowing Sharon to work from home. In fact, the biggest difference between Ted and the CEO who lured Sharon away wasn't the amount of money each man had available to remodel the workplace. The main difference was the *intentionality* each showed in interactions with Sharon. The CEO was listening. And Ted, unfortunately, wasn't.

Here's the bottom line: It's not a collaborative workspace until every member of your team makes a habit of actually *using it* with others to get great work done.

Case Study for the Collaborative Workplace

A fast-growing, entrepreneurially-driven food distribution firm worked with us to design a workspace for a team with a different demographic composition, one that consisted mostly of Millennials.

For that team, we held in-depth discussions with the team before we designed anything. We then created a flexible workspace that used a traditional cubicle layout as the default setting, and used special mobile tables to transform the space into an instant team meeting. When someone hits a roadblock, has a brilliant idea, or needs the input of the group for any reason, the supervisor can pull out the mobile tables, the team members can spin into place on their wheeled chairs, and collaboration kicks into high gear.

It's a great idea... but it's only a great idea because the leader of the team made a point of sharing it with each member of the team ahead of time, and getting full buy-in, *before* setting up the space. He also tested the idea by getting the team's reactions *after* setting up the space, and he then monitored whether the space was actually encouraging people to interact, brainstorm, and solve problems collaboratively. It did!

Remember: If your aim is to create a truly collaborative workspace, you must listen carefully to the team and then be willing to test whether or not people are actually collaborating in the new space! Just coming up with a single good idea and then assuming that your people are connecting with each other is not enough. A collaborative workspace is, by definition, never finished.

Takeaways for the Great Workplace Revolution Coach:

- In a private meeting, ask each member of your team what he or she needs to do the best possible job.

- Listen carefully to the answer(s) you receive.

- Work with each employee to create a workplace that is motivating and makes sense for him or her as an individual. This does not always mean spending a great deal of money, but it must always mean investing personal attention and positive intention.

Great Workplace Revolution Strategy #7: Appoint someone Director of Fun.

KEY CONCEPT: Whether the person is full-time or part-time, paid or unpaid, someone must be personally responsible for helping the organization remember to celebrate.

> *"Just play. Have fun. Enjoy the game."*
>
> — **MICHAEL JORDAN**, former American basketball star

"Why Do We Need a Director of Fun?"

Whenever I begin discussing this part of the Revolution, I start seeing quizzical looks on some people's faces.

When I get to this Workplace Revolution strategy, people sometimes begin to wonder what on earth I'm talking about, whether my business priorities are off, and whether I've taken things just a step too far. People ask: With competition intense, with resources stretched thin, and with customers more demanding than ever, is this seemingly frivolous assignment really all *that* important? Is fun actually a strategic imperative? Does it really need this much time and attention? What if having fun in organized group settings is simply not part of our company culture? And even if fun is as important as I suggest, why on earth can't people be left responsible for having their own fun?

These are all fair questions. At the end of the day, I believe they are all versions of the same question, namely...

IS THIS REALLY ONE OF MY ORGANIZATION'S TOP TWELVE INTERNAL PRIORITIES?

The answer is yes. At least, the answer is yes is if you are serious about launching a Great Workplace Revolution. Here's why. Most workplaces do not inspire loyalty, and a big part of the reason for that is that most workplaces draw a big, uncrossable line between work and pleasure. The basic message most employees receive from their workplaces, the message that gets repeated in countless ways and through countless media, both verbally and nonverbally, both formally and informally, is that "fun is something you do on your own time; work is something you do on our time." This message, however, is an effective obstacle to both creativity and productivity for a significant portion of your workforce. Can you guess why that is?

It's because many of your team members, perhaps most of your team members, received the same numbing, productivity-inhibiting, creativity-destroying message from an institution they eventually came to loathe: school.

Whenever we draw a big black line between work and pleasure, and whenever we guard and defend that line zealously in the workplace, we inevitably summon (unconscious) memories of the strictest, most intimidating teacher that employee ever had. Is that really what we want to do?

Now, it's certainly true that not every creative person on your team had a bad experience in school. It's also true that not every one of your employees sees an unbridgeable division between work and pleasure on the job. And it's also true that, of those who do abide by that "work is not pleasure" doctrine, not every one will disengage and work below potential. *But some creative people will disengage, and* if engaging with those creative employees matters—if you want them contributing, not just taking up space, if it matters to you whether they defect to the competition within the next twelve months—then, yes, making fun a strategic priority is absolutely essential.

How you do that is negotiable. For instance, if your organization's prevailing culture suggests that you call the person who performs this role something other than Director of Fun, that's fine. Whether you make fun in the workplace a top-down priority, however, is not open for discussion... at least, not if you want to implement the system I'm outlining in this book.

"What if having fun in organized group settings is simply not part of our company culture?" I hear this question a lot. In my view, it is always a cop-out, on a personal level, on the organizational level, or on both levels. I realize that the word "cop-out" is a strong one, but in my view it is really the only one that fits. If there are human beings in your workforce, and I'm betting that there are, then there is also some elemental need for celebration and fun. We are wired that way. That need may be expressed in different ways within different organizational cultures, but it must be expressed and supported by senior leaders if you expect to retain the most creative people on your team. To pretend otherwise is to do yourself and your organization a disservice.

When I hear executives tell me that their culture is "incompatible" with having fun in organized group settings, I am tempted to ask: What happens when a senior employee retires or leaves the team? Isn't there some kind of gathering at which people can congregate, honor the person's many contributions, and create a special moment when they can gather together as a group? Have you noticed the sense of renewed purpose and solidarity that often accompanies these meetings? Have you noticed how, for at least an hour or so, the backbiting stops, the arguments recede, the politicking eases, and the focus, attention span, and intentionality of the group improves?

Here's my question: Why wait for someone to retire to realize those organizational benefits?

You don't have to call it "fun" if you don't want to. But you do need to gather the team, put aside the to-do-list, and let people connect with each other as people from time to time. This is true whether your organizational culture is tight, loose, creative, disciplined, or indefinable!

> You've spent enough time reading about this! Throw a party! Now! Have some fun!

The ability to identify someone with direct personal responsibility for creating official, company-sponsored opportunities for fun is the acid test for your organization's real-world commitment to create, support, and reward a culture of celebration. No Great Workplace Revolution is possible without that kind of culture.

You can tell a lot about the true intentions of any organization's claims to be a Great Place to Work ... just by checking in to find out who's formally in charge of finding reasons for the team to have a party. Remember: The Director of Fun may have any number of possible job titles and may have any number of additional responsibilities on the job description. At the end of the day, however, he or she must be the person who is individually accountable for identifying the best reasons, and ways, to launch a celebration.

Case Study for a Director of Fun: The Scooter Store

The Texas-based scooter and power chair manufacturer known as The Scooter Store employs a VP of Celebration who schedules dozens of company-sponsored celebrations annually. These range from an all-employee cruise to something as simple—but profoundly important—as finding ways to mark employee birthdays and anniversaries.

According to the company's website, "One of the Scooter Store's Core Ideologies is 'Have Fun.' The Scooter Store is committed to making the workplace enjoyable and celebrating the accomplishments, large and small, of its customers and employee-owners."

If you're curious about the bottom-line impact of this workplace philosophy, which has been woven into the company's cultural DNA from the company's very earliest days, check out the numbers. After having been founded from a single store location in 1991, The Scooter Store is now an industry leader, having grown to 129 locations across the United States. It now employs more than 2,000 people, and serves over more than 400,000 customers. The company's annual revenue is estimated at over $300 million. The Scooter Store made FORTUNE Magazine's 2010 list of the 100 Best Companies to Work for in America.

Follow The Scooter Store's lead and appoint someone as Director of Fun today!

Takeaways for the Great Workplace Revolution Coach:

- Appoint one person in your organization as Director of Fun. (As Great Workplace Revolution Coach, you yourself may be the best candidate, at least initially.)
- Call this person by whatever title seems most relevant and appropriate to your organization.
- Start scheduling and holding events that build and reinforce a culture of celebration.

Great Workplace Revolution Strategy #8: Create after-work events that involve direct personal contact with customers and employees.

KEY CONCEPT: Off-site events build team cohesion and remind your people why they're doing what they're doing.

THE GREAT WORKPLACE REVOLUTION

"One of the deep secrets of life is that all that is really worth doing Is what we do for others."

— **LEWIS CARROLL** (1832–1898), author best known for writing *Alice in Wonderland*

Chicago-based Soliant Consulting is a leading specialist in helping businesses to customize and exploit the power and flexibility of the database software FileMaker Pro. Soliant's team has decades of experience and one of the deepest benches of talent in the world; members of the team have won an unprecedented four FileMaker Excellence Awards, have co-authored six books, have spoken at each annual FileMaker Developer Conference for the past ten years, and have written white papers and industry articles for major publications.

Bob Bowers, CEO of Soliant Consulting, shared some insights on the vital importance of sponsoring off-site group events that are not (directly) related to the attainment of work objectives. There is a fascinating paradox at work here. Although the team-driven events his company arranges outside the workplace are not tied to the completion of specific projects, they are still an essential part of the team approach that makes success in the workplace possible. They are as important as anything else the company does.

"We're very team-focused," Bob told me during our interview. "Everything I do, really, is to try to reinforce that. We've used a lot of bonus and incentive programs and the ones I like the best are team-oriented and not individual. We use various events outside the workplace to make collaboration and support of the team a reality during the work day. We're always looking for events that can connect individual team members more closely to the groups that they work with. We use these as team-building exercises, where people can learn the art and skill of pulling together and supporting each other.

"We're also trying to make a place where people enjoy showing up each day. It's not just about work here. We know people have to have interests outside of work. If we're going to be spending this much time together working then we should at least find a way to enjoy each other's company. Doing that on a regular basis builds a good team atmosphere.

"Off-site events are just one of the ways we embody the values of our organization, but they're an incredibly important part. For instance, we have created non-project-related engineering challenges, which are basically engineering puzzles that we get to solve outside of the office environment. We're a bunch of programmers, so this is something that appeals to us. This kind of challenge usually involves splitting into teams of five or six people doing some sort of competition.

"One year we went out and built sandcastles on a wet, rainy day. We were all soaking wet and laughing and tired, and we built these giant sandcastles. We had someone from the hotel judge which one was the best. It was just a great afternoon.

"Another year, we did something with programmable Lego blocks. These are Lego blocks that can actually obey commands. We had a massive sumo competition with sumo wrestling robots we had built from Legos. That made a big impression.

"We've also had competitions where you had to build bridges out of toothpicks and glue. We always try to keep it simple, using simple materials. It's good to get off-site and spend an afternoon in a thinking activity where you have to come up with an inventive or novel way of solving a problem as a team. It kicks things off, it gets people talking to each other, and it's a fun way for everyone to get to know each other a little better.

"In addition to those kinds of competitions, we also hold events where we spend time going over the performance of the company for the past year. We generally have two days where we gather everyone from our offices into one spot, and I'll talk about our performance over the last year and our objectives and goals for the next year. We try to include some kind of professional development activity, such as bringing in an outside speaker, but for a lot of people on the team, one of the biggest highlight of this gathering is the annual talent show.

"This has become an important tradition for us. We've got a very creative bunch, and it turns out that a lot of us are very musical. Here's how it got started: We were looking for something to do on the Monday night of this annual event, and I said, 'Well, how about we do an open mike sort of thing? People can come up on stage and do something or play something, and I'll bring my guitar, and we'll see what happens.' There were very low expectations for that first year, but I asked a couple of our developers to organize it and they kind of ran with it and they did an outstanding job. They booked the hotel and had one of the rooms transformed into kind of a nightclub setting, with tables and candles and a little sound stage. People brought microphones and whatnot, and suddenly we had a great little area for this event, and it just took off from there. The whole team just had a great time with it, and we had all these different acts and saw new sides of every team member who participated.

"This was one of those things that no one expected would be that big a deal, but after the first talent show, everyone you talked to was saying, 'Wow, that was really neat. We had no idea how talented our co-workers were.' It wasn't necessarily that people were great musicians but just that they felt comfortable enough to share a side of themselves that they didn't normally share in their work life. I also think it was a good advantage for me as the boss to get up there with my guitar and show them a side of myself that they don't get to see at the job, and kind of serve as a role model. But I certainly wasn't the only role model. We've got one developer here who's basically a professional opera singer; he was our master of ceremonies, and he sang an aria at the end of the night which was just phenomenal. But we also had one guy who had been taking guitar lessons for about ten weeks and only knew two chords. He brought his guitar in and sat up there on stage and said, 'Hey, every-body, I've only been playing for ten weeks. You guys have to help me out here by singing along.' He picked a song everyone knew, he strummed the two chords, and he had to pause once in a while as he was changing chords, but everyone was singing along and everyone was rooting for him, so proud that he could get up there and share his talent with the rest of the team there. It was really quite a wonderful experience."

Takeaways for the Great Workplace Revolution Coach:

- Use regular off-site activities to build a sense of team cohesion and support.

- Make sure the events are not directly associated with the achievement of any workplace goal.

- Consider sponsoring two kinds of off-site events: those that play to your team's existing skill sets (such as a sandcastle contest for engineers) and those that show a different, unexpected side of each individual (such as a talent show).

Great Workplace Revolution Strategy #9: Give something back to the community.

KEY CONCEPT: Group-driven charitable activities engage the team, build loyalty to the organization, and fatten the bottom line.

> *"If I am not for myself, who will be for me? If I am not for others, what am I? And if not now, when?"*
>
> — **RABBI HILLEL**, one of the most important
> figures in Jewish history

Giving Something Back

A lot of people are surprised to find the principle of coordinated, company-sponsored charitable giving on the list of principles supporting a Great Workplace Revolution. As with Strategy #8, many people are a bit uncertain about how this initiative contributes to the attainment of financial goals. A friend of mine recalled recently that a manger he once worked for told him bluntly, "Charity is fine if it's something you want to do on your own, but we don't invest company resources in that kind of thing." End of discussion!

If you are a leader who is resistant to the idea that company-sponsored charitable activity can and does improve the bottom line, this section of the book will be a particularly important one for you to read. If you work for such a person, you may simply want to reproduce the list below (you have my permission to do so) and then post it somewhere your boss can see it.

Five Reasons It Helps Your Organization's Bottom Line to Sponsor a Charitable Event Outside of the Workplace

1. It builds team cohesion like nothing else. Team members who collaborate once a quarter (or even more frequently) on an

off-site charitable event, in my experience, have significantly better attitudes toward the members of their own team, and also toward the members of other teams with whom they must interact from time to time.

2. It gets your salespeople exposure to major new business opportunities. Volunteering is a proven, but often overlooked, prospecting strategy, one that often leads to direct personal relationships with critical senior-level contacts.

3. It improves staff retention. Try it on a quarterly basis for twelve months and see for yourself!

4. It gives you a bigger base of contacts from which to recruit talented new employees. In this area, as well, charitable events give you and your organization unsurpassed networking opportunities.

5. It makes people more likely to come in early and stay late— on their own initiative—when working on critical projects. Again, try it for a year and compare the numbers.

Case Study for Giving Something Back: Zimmerman Advertising

Florida-based advertising agency Zimmerman Advertising is one of the most successful and prominent outfits in the country. In the essay below, reprinted by permission, CEO and founder Jordan Zimmerman explains how he assigned his team a new "client": Piper High School.

Back to School: A Lesson for Grownups

"Our educational system is failing American kids. I believe it is up to successful business people to step in, make a difference, and help give students a fighting chance. That's why, a couple of years ago, I got involved with Piper High School in Sunrise, Florida, through Florida's Partnership to Advance School Success (PASS) via the Denise and Jordan Zimmerman Family Foundation, whose slant is towards kids and education.

"I should mention that Piper is my old high school. It is part of the Broward County School District, and it faces a lot of challenges. The Florida school grading system awards a letter grade to each school based on students' standardized test performance; Piper is a 'C' school. One-third of the kids didn't graduate last year. Almost half of the students qualify for the free lunch program.

"I adopted Piper and made a three-year financial commitment, as well as a commitment to collaborate one-on-one with Piper's principal, Enid Valdez, to improve the school. Our goal: Make the classes more interesting and relevant, and try to inspire more students to start thinking about what could be. We started making a difference.

"Most recently, I saw one area where I felt the Zimmerman team could make an immediate impact on the students: the video facilities. Principal Valdez agreed with me on this. She told me that, whenever she received feedback from students on the Piper television course, there was a great deal of frustration and disappointment. It was hard to keep the program alive, because the school just didn't have the tools it needed to produce good new video content.

"It does now. The Zimmerman Advertising team visited the site and gave Piper the video production equipment it needed; then, as a team, we worked through the summer to redesign the space for teacher Jovan Conde's Television Production class. The new, completely revamped TV rooms include a new set with a green screen, state-of-the-art Panasonic cameras equipped with teleprompters, and all the latest editing and production equipment. The kids at Piper, and the great teachers and administrators there, now have a professional-level production facility. Approximately 100 Piper students have enrolled in the four TV Production class levels. Members of our team are also helping to teach the course.

"Principal Valdez is not exaggerating when she says a class like this can literally keep a student from dropping out... and serve as a beacon to hundreds of other kids who don't take the video class, but do see its output.

"This is not just about writing checks, but about working hand-in-hand, as a team, with a local school and local officials, up to and including the mayor of Sunrise, Mike Ryan. Together, we are making a huge difference for the students. We are now going to send in some of our executives to teach some classes!

"August 22 was a big day. It was not only the first day of school for kids at Piper, but also the day that the new video facility was up and running. I hope those kids are not the only ones who learned something new and exciting on that day, though. I hope every grownup who's in a position to make a contribution of time or money to a public school takes a lesson from what just happened at Piper... and learns what we as a team have learned about the many benefits of giving something back to the community."

Can you make a difference in one school's ability to engage and educate its kids? How? When are you going to start?

> Giving back to the community is the ultimate teambuilding initiative!

Takeaways for the Great Workplace Revolution Coach:

- **Find a charitable cause your that your whole team can make an off-site time commitment to *as a group.***

- Make sure everyone on the team is engaged and ready to help.

- Set the time and date, gather the team, and get to work!

Great Workplace Revolution Strategy #10: Ensure that each employee's work space makes good ergonomic sense.

KEY CONCEPT: Building and sustaining user-friendly workplaces always enhances efficiency, productivity, and profitability.

"The human body has physical limitations.... Workers feel the effects of (ergonomic stress) physically and emotionally through aches, pains, and strains. Employers feel the effects through increased workers' compensation claims, high medical costs, lost workdays, and an overall decrease in worker productivity."

— Ergodyne.com

Ergonomics is defined as "the applied science of equipment design, as for the workplace, intended to maximize productivity by reducing operator fatigue and discomfort." Most businesses don't make much of an investment of time or money in making sure each employee's physical working environment fits like a glove, and that's a shame, because the impact of ergonomics is hard to overstate. Here's a brief glimpse of what's at stake.

Repetitive motion illness and cumulative trauma disorders, classic ergonomic disorders, represent almost half of all occupational illnesses reported by the Bureau of Labor Statistics. Although cost estimates vary greatly, it is believed that medical and workers' compensation costs of ergonomic disorders exceed $100 billion annually. Our company, Thomas Interior Systems, is dedicated to helping clients improve their office environments. To do this, we utilize a physical therapist who specializes in office ergonomics and has trained hundreds of individuals to reduce their exposure to risk factors at work.

A workstation that is properly adjusted to meet individual ergonomic needs will enhance the health, safety and comfort of a worker—and, I believe, improve that worker's capacity for productive, creative work. That's more than enough to get any Great Workplace Revolution Coach started, but if you need additional incentives, consider the lost productivity, workers' compensation claims, and potential legal liability you will have to deal with if you make a habit of ignoring this issue!

Case Study for Intelligent Ergonomic Assessment: Thomas Interior Systems

We advise the use of the following questionnaire to assess whether an employee's workstation components fit properly. Here's where we walk our talk: We make sure that our own employees use this checklist to ensure a good ergonomic fit... and if there are any "no" answers to the questions below, we change the work environment until the answer is "yes"!

Seating:

1. When you sit in your chair, are your feet flat on the floor?
2. Are your shoulders relaxed with your chair armrests at the proper height?
3. Does your chair have lumbar support that is easy to adjust?
4. Can you adjust the seat and backrest if needed?
5. Does your chair tilt or swivel to allow you to adjust your seating posture?

Keyboard or Mouse:

1. Is your keyboard positioned directly in front of you?

2. Is the mouse close by and easy to reach?

3. Can you use the mouse and keyboard without bending or reaching?

4. Can you keep your wrists and hands straight when you work?

Monitor:

1. Is your monitor positioned directly in front of you so that you can see it without turning your head?

2. Is the top of the monitor at or below your eye level and can you adjust the angle?

3. Is the monitor approximately an arm's length away (about 20")?

Work Space:

1. Are the items you use in front of you and close by?

2. Can you turn and easily reach what you need in your work-station?

3. Can your thighs fit comfortably underneath your work surface?

4. Can you move your feet and legs freely?

Accessories:

1. Is your document holder close by?

2. If you use wrist supports, are they padded?

3. Do your wrist supports keep your hands and forearms straight?

4. Can you use your telephone without bending your head or raising your shoulder?

Working Conditions:

1. Do you use a keyboard or mouse for less than 4 hours a day?

2. Are your back, neck, or wrists bent for less than 2 hours in one day?

3. Do you take micro breaks when performing prolonged tasks?

4. Have you been trained in ergonomic principles?

I hope you and all your team members were able to answer "yes" to all of these questions. If you didn't, and you have questions on how to set up an ergonomic workspace, please feel free to contact me personally via the Thomas Interior Systems website.

Takeaways for the Great Workplace Revolution Coach:

- Conduct a personalized ergonomic assessment for each of your organization's employee at least once a year.

- Make all necessary adjustments and changes in the physical workspace.

- For help and guidance with specific ergonomic issues, contact Thomas Interior Systems.

Great Workplace Revolution Strategy #11: Invest in ongoing education and personal development.

KEY CONCEPT: Creative people stick around longer, and make more important contributions, when you support their learning and personal development goals.

"Change and growth take place when a person has risked himself and dares to become involved with experimenting with his own life."

— **HERBERT A. OTTO**, psychologist

Case Study for Investing in Personal and Professional Development: The Walt Disney Companies

One of America's truly great, visionary entrepreneurs, Walt Disney, proved his personal commitment to the ongoing educational and personal and professional development of his staff during some of the darkest days of the Great Depression. Disney paid to make sure his animators could take art classes, and he did so at a time when his company was experiencing major cash flow problems! Some of Disney's business allies (bankers among them) saw this as an unpardonable extravagance, given the company's financial situation, but Walt Disney insisted on investing in the personal growth of his key creative staff. The payoff for his company? *Snow White and the Seven Dwarfs*... among other masterpieces!

The Disney commitment to personal and professional development continues to this day, and is one of Disney's greatest legacies to the company that bears his name. Seven decades on, take a look at the enduring legacy of the Disney organization's commitment to continuing education, the investment that keeps on giving in both the workplace and the marketplace:

"Disney University provides Walt Disney World's 42,000 cast members with world-class training in diverse skills ranging from computer applications to culinary arts to regulatory training. The Disney University Cast Member Catalog rivals some community college catalogs in size and scope. In addition, cast members are also eligible to participate in the company's Educational Reimbursement Plan, which allows cast members to attend courses to pursue a college education at Disney's expense. Disney's model includes the utilization of Mobile Training Units to allow workers to have access to computer training at their worksite, when it's most convenient for them. In addition, Disney allows training via satellite to some of the top business schools in the United States for mid- and upper-level management. But Disney's model goes far beyond offering continuing education to employees. Largely regarded as a leader in customer service and business, Disney has developed a rather passionate following in the business world. Leaders across a wide variety of industries want to learn the "Mickey Mouse" business model. So Disney University expanded to accommodate demand, developing the Disney University Professional Development Programs, enabling them to train business men and women in such subjects as people management, creative leadership, and quality service, while turning a nice profit from derivative revenue in the process." (Source: *The Benefits and Methods of Continuing Employee Education*, published by 4imprint.com.)

"Training" Is For Seals!

Continuing education takes place *inside* the workplace as well, of course. How that education takes place, including the language we use to describe it, matters a great deal. At Thomas Interior Systems, we work with a lot of organizations that ask us for our help and guidance in designing and setting up things like a "training room," a "training center," or even (if customers are looking for assistance with their curriculum development) the specifics of their "training program."

There is evidence of a huge internal problem built into each of those requests. Can you spot it?

"Training" is a loaded word. It implies dominance and removes the possibility of a peer-to-peer relationship. Training is what animal wranglers do to make performing seals do a better job of balancing colored balls on their noses. Training is not—or at any rate shouldn't be—what peers who respect one another do to each other in the workplace!

What are we really doing when we bring a group, large or small, into the so-called "training room"? Supporting ongoing growth and education? Yes. Sharing important best practices? Absolutely. Sharing critical market intelligence? You bet.

Training? I don't think so. That word implies the rote repetition of certain habitual actions that have been drilled into the trainee. It certainly doesn't imply support of independent thought, critical analysis, or implementation of the creative process. If we want to attract and retain employees who think for themselves, who ask essential questions that others have overlooked, or who bring innovative new solutions to the workplace, we must stop using terminology that treats them like performing seals!

I firmly believe that this is one of those areas of workplace life where the terminology we choose to use has a direct impact—for better or for worse—on the overall workplace experience of our employees. The fact that we are used to using a certain term definitely DOES NOT mean that that term belongs on the workplace lexicon. In the case of "training," I believe we can instantly improve workplace morale by simply replacing the word.

Does your organization currently have "training initiatives"? What would happen if you rechristened them "learning initiatives"? Does it "train people" in effective communication, selling, or anything else? What would happen if it "shared proven best practices" instead?

At the end of the day, the word you use to replace the word "training" doesn't matter as much as the organizational decision to remove the word from your organizational vocabulary. For instance, at our company, we decided to create a "learning center" rather than a "training center." That's because we believe that this place is where people come to learn, not where they come to be trained! That's the decision that worked for us... but I urge you to make your own decision today.

Takeaways for the Great Workplace Revolution Coach:

- Make a long-term commitment to the personal and professional development of every employee—or, at the very least, the personal and professional development of the employees you hope to retain.

- Stop talking about "training." Find another word.

- Make learning initiatives—both work-related and life-skill-related—one of the defining experiences of working for your company.

Great Workplace Revolution Strategy #12: Give employees regular feedback.

KEY CONCEPT: With good communication, a true Workplace Revolution becomes much easier; without it, such a revolution is impossible.

> *"We believe we do a better job at giving feedback than we really do."*

> — **RICK MAURER**, change management consultant, expert, speaker and bestselling author

Case Study: Rethinking the Employee Performance Evaluation at the Land Of Nod

The Land of Nod (www.landofnod.com) is an innovative catalog, Internet, and retail store operation that specializes in imaginatively crafted children's furniture, bedding, and accessories. The company, which designs the majority of its own items, was founded from a humble home basement by partners Scott Eirinberg and Jamie Cohen in 1996; in 2000, Eirinberg and Cohen agreed to an equity partnership with Crate & Barrel to help expand the firm's US reach.

I sat down with cofounder and CEO Jamie Cohen to talk about one of his favorite subjects: how to help employees grow personally and professionally on the job by giving them the right feedback during formal assessment sessions.

Tom: You used to be a big believer in what the rest of the world calls a "standard performance evaluation," as I understand it?

Jamie: Yes. For about the first four years of our company's existence, I followed the standard procedure that I knew pretty much every other organization in America was following. That was to schedule regular performance reviews with every employee in the organization—which I still think is a great idea—and then to build those reviews around my own two-part written assessment of how I felt the employee was doing. Part One was all about strengths, and Part Two was all about weaknesses, although I, like lots of other people, came up with various euphemisms to cover up the word "weakness."

Tom: And that two-part structure was eventually something that you as a leader decided to change at the Land of Nod, correct?

Jamie: That's right.

Tom: How come?

Jamie: Because I realized that I was running into the same issues over and over again with certain employees, and I realized that other people in our company were having the same problem. So at some point, you need to step back and ask why that is. Now, ideally, the performance review process should be an opportunity to clear the air, to give employees a sense of engagement, to give them a sense that it's their turn. But we realized that there were obstacles standing in the way of that happening. People kept getting the same issues in the "weakness" column, review after review, year after year.

Tom: And why was that, do you think?

Jamie: Because the employees were smart enough to figure out the dynamic of the review session. After only one or two of those evaluation meetings, they quickly grasped what was happening. They knew that the supervisor was going to start out with the good stuff, the strengths that they had shown on the job over the past six months. And they also learned that the good stuff was inevitably going to turn into the discussion of the weaknesses, which they perceived as the real reason for the meeting, no matter what euphemisms we put on the second section. A lot of people, including me, were having trouble getting the idea across that this was actually meant to be constructive criticism. Employees usually concluded that the criticism really didn't feel constructive at all. They came to see the whole exercise as a way for them to get beaten down by management. So they got frustrated. And they tuned out. No matter what labels we put on that second section of the supervisor's evaluation, the meeting usually created a conflict-oriented environment. So I decided to try something different.

Tom: So is it fair to say that you that you had an "aha" moment? That at some point you knew you needed to do something different with regard to personnel evaluation at Land of Nod, something that went beyond the classic "Here's what I see as your strengths, here's what I see as your weaknesses" discussion with employees?

Jamie: Well, yes and no. There was no single "aha" moment. What happened was we decided over time that the classic evaluation agenda, the one where you lead with a discussion of what went right, and then follow up with a discussion of what went wrong, actually had a pretty limited application. Now, to be fair, this model is actually quite useful for a lot of the people who are just getting started in their careers, for the workers who may be brand new to the idea of going to a workplace and collaborating with colleagues on a project, for employees who are perhaps learning what the job expectations are for the first time, and how those expectations might differ from the ones you find a school environment. So for the first few scheduled evaluation meetings of someone's career, that classic two-part format can actually be a great tool. But what we found was that for people who had been around a little longer and had a little more experience, that model was a roadblock. People got tired of hearing about the same few problems over and over, maybe for two or three years straight. And occasionally, supervisors were relying too heavily on that two-part tool as a platform for their own monologues, rather than as an opportunity for dialogue with the employee. So we knew we were missing opportunities for growth. For a variety of reasons, there was the possibility of some resentment and some baggage building up, and a lot of people were anticipating getting into conflict mode whenever they walked into their evaluations.

Tom: So how did you change the dynamic for those more experienced employees?

Jamie: Well, I started out by thinking about the person who keeps getting the same notes about the same areas for improvement over and over again. I said to myself, "Let's assume, for the sake of argument, that the supervisor is right about those areas that he or she thinks the employee needs to improve. What is going on there?" And the answer I came up with was that the reason the person was not improving was not that he or she was a bad employee, but rather that the person had encountered some kind of block that was preventing personal growth and progress as a person. And I realized that, if we wanted to bring about real behavioral change, if we really wanted the person to grow, we had to have more of an open-ended discussion, not a scripted exchange. We had to turn it into something more like a personal coaching session, and we had to have real dialogue.

Tom: And how did you launch that?

Jamie: I started with my own senior executives, the people who reported directly to me. I told them I was throwing out the old two-part format, because I didn't think it was doing either of us any good, and I told them that, from this point forward, I was going to need more participation and more analysis from their side during these evaluation sessions. I told them that they were actually going to be doing their own evaluations and drawing their own conclusions. They would be evaluating themselves using their own methods, and I would offer them some insights and reality checks on their conclusions. I told them that, from this point forward, I considered myself a coach, someone who was tasked with helping them to move forward in their career. And then I asked them where they thought we should start.

Tom: And what was the response?

Jamie: The response was dramatically positive from every single person. Suddenly they were engaged, and the conflict dynamic was gone. I saw first-hand that the new starting-point for the meeting instantly put the supervisor and the employee on the same side. I've now been using this method for four years with my own direct reports, and have gotten really great results with it.

Tom: Were there any specific phrases you would recommend that supervisors who are trying to implement this evaluation approach use when they try this for the first time?

Jamie: Yes. It's extremely important that you make it clear that the new discussions are impartial, unbiased, and not in any way connected to some goal that benefits only the employer. The sentence that has evolved for doing that over the last four years sounds something like this: "Look, we are on your side, and the only reason for holding these meetings now is to help you to move forward in your career and reach your full potential... whether that's with this company or with someone else." And, of course, I mean that. Now, saying that out loud and really meaning it, making eye contact at that moment, all helps me to land the point that there are no ulterior motives. That's what starts people thinking about what their full potential really might be. The whole purpose of the evaluation process from that moment onward is now to get people curious about how they could change for the better... and if they're not changing for the better right now, why not.

Tom: So how did you know for sure that the new, open-ended coaching discussion was a more effective feedback tool for your more experienced employees than the old "strengths and weaknesses"?

Jamie: People started making progress. They started becoming more curious about how to identify and overcome their own obstacles.

And they started breaking through those obstacles. Suddenly, when you took away the perceived dynamic of making a list of things the employee had done wrong, and you started telling the employee, "Hey, I'm here for you, I want you to be able to reach your full potential, whether it's here with us or with another employer"—when you did that, the whole dynamic of the review meeting changed. The employees started taking the lead in figuring out what needed to change, and how it was going to change, and when, and why.

Tom: Can you give us an example?

Jamie: I had one particular direct report who had consistently gotten notes on her personnel review about communication problems. Previously, I think she had seen all of those notes from me about communication as white noise, as something she was just going to tune out, because it didn't really mean anything to her. I kept bringing it up, and it kept not changing. But with the new format, I was able to play the role of her personal coach, and ask her, "So what do you think is going on here? It seems like there are times when your communication suffers when you have a lot to do. I think some of the people who report to you would say that you might not be at your best when you're under pressure. What's your feeling about that?"

And in the context of a coaching session, her response was 180 degrees different from what it had been. Now she wanted to get to the bottom of what was going on, she wanted to come up with a plan for changing the behavior. She really wanted to be able to show me that she had made progress in her communication skills.

Tom: And did she?

Jamie: She absolutely did. She figured out when and where and why these ineffective communications were happening most often. She began to look, on her own, for strategies that would help her to communicate better with her team and with me. She also figured out some ways to prepare her own team for those occasional lapses we all have when things get hectic. The result is that she is now a much better communicator in the workplace. Both she and her team have a better sense of humor and a better ongoing rapport about communications issues. More to the point, she has taken over personal responsibility for her own assessment review process. She is in charge of her own performance, and her own growth in the position. She is now looking for new areas to grow. It's a much more healthy and viable process for everyone involved.

Tom: Is that kind of positive response from an employee typical, in your experience, when you move out of the traditional personnel assessment model, and into the coaching sessions you describe?

Jamie: Absolutely.

Tom: So what are your plans now with regard to the performance review process at Land of Nod? What have you learned from all this?

Jamie: We are in the process of pushing the new coaching-driven process into other areas of the organization. So far, everywhere we have used it, we've gotten dramatic positive results.

Takeaways for the Great Workplace Revolution Coach:

- Focus more on coaching for long-term success and less on passing out "strength and weakness" grades during performance evaluation sessions.

- Tie performance evaluations to your organization's list of core values. (See Strategy #1.)

- Make it clear to your employees that you want them to succeed in their careers, preferably with your organization, but with any other employer they should end up working for if they happen to find another career path.

PART FOUR:
CONCISE SUMMARY FOR THE GREAT WORKPLACE REVOLUTION COACH

If you are the Great Workplace Revolution Coach, my challenge to you is a simple one: Post this to-do list in your workplace, where you can see it every day... and take action on it!

Takeaways for the Great Workplace Revolution Coach

Great Workplace Revolution Strategy #1:
Identify the organization's core values and talk about those values frequently with customers and employees.

- Work with senior management, and the enterprise as a whole, to identify a list of core values. The list should reflect the values that your very best people already follow.

- Take your time.

- Engage the team as you refine and finalize the list. The final list should be the conclusion of an in-depth conversation, not a one-way "things-had-better-change-around-here" memo.

- Use the list of core values to help in day-to-day decisions and to confirm hiring standards.

Great Workplace Revolution Strategy #2:
Design and constantly refine a creative work space based on direct employee feedback.

- Use major (or minor!) changes in workplace environment design as opportunities to communicate with your team, to discuss the changes you have in mind, and to collect good design ideas from your people.

- As in the values discussion (see Strategy #1), engage the team as you refine and finalize the design. The final design should be the conclusion of an in-depth conversation.

- Emphasize design elements of the workplace that have multiple uses, and look for new ways spaces can be configured to serve multiple purposes. A flexible, adaptive, creative physical workspace is one of the best ways to attract, support, and retain a flexible, adaptive, and creative team.

Great Workplace Revolution Strategy #3:
Put the right person in the right job.

- Visit Kolbe.com and get yourself assessed so that you can identify and capitalize on your own conative strengths.

- Then, get your team assessed so that you can identify and help them capitalize on their conative strengths.

- Advocate for the use of the Kolbe assessment system at all levels of your organization.

Great Workplace Revolution Strategy #4:
Provide constant accommodation to, and understanding of, the whole employee.

- Make sure supervisors know the first names (at least) of each of their direct reports' close family members. Start this trend by learning about your own direct reports' families!

- Be supportive when challenges arise in an employee's home

life. Give employees the benefit of the doubt when deciding when and how to offer support.

- Show high person-to-person intentionality regardless of the size of your budget.

Great Workplace Revolution Strategy #5:
Build appropriate recognition for a job well done into the culture.

- Create a system for recognition of individual employee achievements and accomplishments.

- Build this system around timed messages (for instance, every three months, every six months, or every year, based on what you feel is right for your organization) or around the attainment of specific performance targets (such as closing a sale of a certain size or receiving high marks for customer satisfaction)

- As you design, test, and implement your system, bear in mind that even though most people enjoy public praise and recognition, some people don't. Make sure there are alternative forms of recognition for team members who would prefer to have their accomplishments acknowledged privately.

Great Workplace Revolution Strategy #6:
Support a truly collaborative workplace, both physically and emotionally.

- In a private meeting, ask each member of your team what he or she needs to do the best possible job.

- Listen carefully to the answer(s) you receive.

- Work with each employee to create a workplace that is motivating and makes sense for him or her as an individual. This does not always mean spending a great deal of money, but it must always mean investing personal attention and positive intention.

Great Workplace Revolution Strategy #7:
Appoint someone Director of Fun.

- Appoint one person in your organization as Director of Fun. (As Great Workplace Revolution Coach, you yourself may be the best candidate, at least initially.)

- Call this person by whatever title seems most relevant and appropriate to your organization.

- Start scheduling and holding events that build and reinforce a culture of celebration.

Great Workplace Revolution Strategy #8:
Create after-work events that involve direct personal contact with customers and employees.

- Use regular off-site activities to build a sense of team cohesion and support.

- Make sure the events are not directly associated with the achievement of any workplace goal.

- Consider sponsoring two kinds of off-site events: those that play to your team's existing skill sets (such as a sandcastle contest for engineers) and those that show a different, unexpected side of each individual (such as a talent show).

Great Workplace Revolution Strategy #9:
Give something back to the community.

- Find a charitable cause your that your whole team can make an off-site time commitment to *as a group*.

- Make sure everyone on the team is engaged and ready to help.

- Set the time and date, gather the team, and get to work!

Great Workplace Revolution Strategy #10:
Ensure that each employee's work space makes good ergonomic sense.

- Conduct a personalized ergonomic assessment for each of your organization's employee at least once a year.

- Make all necessary adjustments and changes in the physical workspace.

- For help and guidance with specific ergonomic issues, contact Thomas Interior Systems.

Great Workplace Revolution Strategy #11:
Invest in ongoing education and personal development.

- Make a long-term commitment to the personal and professional development of every employee or, at the very least, the personal and professional development of the employees you hope to retain.

- Stop talking about "training." Find another word.

- Make learning initiatives—both work-related and life-skill-related—one of the defining experiences of working for your company.

Great Workplace Revolution Strategy #12:
Give employees regular feedback.

- Focus more on coaching for long-term success and less on

passing out "strength and weakness" grades during performance evaluation sessions.

- Tie performance evaluations to your organization's list of core values. (See Strategy #1.)

- Make it clear to your employees that you want them to succeed in their careers, preferably with your organization, but with any other employer they should end up working for if they happen to find another career path.

EPILOGUE:
THREE REASONS COMPLACENCY IS NOT AN OPTION

"Providence has its appointed hour for everything. We cannot command results, we can only strive. But we must strive."

— **MAHATMA GANDHI** (1869–1948), political and ideological leader of the independence movement in India

"A boss creates fear, a leader confidence. A boss fixes blame, a leader corrects mistakes. A boss knows all, a leader asks questions. A boss makes work drudgery, a leader makes it interesting. A boss is interested in himself or herself, a leader is interested in the group."

— **RUSSELL EWING**, British journalist

And now it's time for you to change the status quo, either because you must change your own role or because you already have a good program up and running and you know that it must constantly change and evolve to keep your team on the cutting edge. There is no part of this program where you get to sit back and watch.

Whichever of the two categories you fall into, I am asking you now to take the initiative to shake things up within your organization. I know that changing the status quo is always a challenge. Implementing the twelve Great Workplace strategies I outline in this book is hard work. Taking action is not going to be as easy as doing nothing, and taking action will demand that you overcome the strong temptation of continuing to run your business in the way that is most familiar to you.

You may convince yourself that following the path of least resistance in your workplace will at least get you something close to the results you have gotten used to receiving, or that launching a revolution in the workplace is something optional, something you can do later on, if you feel like it, if things calm down and you aren't quite as busy. The truth, however, is more sobering, and less accommodating. The truth is that you have no choice. Complacency in the coming years will lead to a spiral of failure. Continuing to do what is familiar will cost time, resources, and people that you simply cannot afford to lose in the current environment.

Launching a Great Workplace Revolution is not an optional undertaking you should commit yourself to when you have solved all the other problems, when the dust settles and you have ample time and money set aside. It is a major strategic imperative that demands at least some of your available attention every single working day.

There are three big reasons why implementing the twelve Great Workplace strategies is not something you can put off until tomorrow. These aren't the only reasons, of course, but they are the ones that I predict you'll find hardest to forget.

ONE: Your most creative employees are going to notice if you don't launch this revolution—a revolution where everybody wins. You will equip them, get them ready for great things, and then watch them walk out the door as they go do those great things somewhere else.

TWO: Your competition is going to notice if you don't launch a revolution. These may be competitors you know about, or they may be operating in some far-flung location you've never heard of. Regardless, they will take advantage, directly or indirectly, of the talent leaving your organization, and will create (or adapt) products and services that cut into your market and make it harder for you to stay in business.

THREE: Your customers are *definitely* going to notice if you don't launch a revolution. One of the things you will notice as you implement these twelve strategies is a simple, predictable, and powerful formula that plays out to your organization's benefit time and time again: CUSTOMERS ESTABLISH LONG-TERM RELATIONSHIPS WITH COMPANIES WHOSE EMPLOYEES HAVE A LONG-TERM COMMITMENT TO THE MISSION. The converse, however is also true: Companies whose most creative employees *do not* have an enduring commitment to the organization will have a harder time holding on to customers.

If any one of these reasons gives you pause—and all three should— then you are ready to make the commitment to take action, today, to implement these twelve strategies.

Before we close the main section of this book, I have to share a few thoughts on the process of developing this material, which has truly been a labor of love for me and my team. In one sense, about a year of work has gone into writing this manuscript. In another sense, though, it's really something I've been working on for my whole professional life, a fulfillment of our company's ongoing mission and vision: TO IMPROVE THE OFFICE WORK ENVIRONMENT.

Often, over the past year, I have been fortunate enough to be able to talk about the twelve Great Workplace Revolution strategies in front of many groups of people curious about the subject of workplace engagement. One of the most common questions I get from those groups is some variation on the classic, skeptical query: "What's in it for me?" In other words, what's the payoff, personally and organizationally, for rebuilding an organization around these twelve strategies? The answer is pretty simple, and by now I hope it is second nature to you: When you make your employees #1, you create a workforce of happy, creative employees. You need that kind of workforce if you plan to keep your customers happy. Superior customer service is the end result of this revolution where everyone wins!

Don't put off launching that revolution for a minute longer. Don't wait until you have all the money you need, all the time you want, or all the market share you'd like before you get started. Do what we did at our company. When we started this program, we didn't have money, time, or market share... but we did what we could with what was in front of us to build a great workplace. Now it's time for you to do the same.

> Start now! Do what you can with what you have today!

Please stay in touch! E-mail me about the journey, and the lessons you learn along the way. You can reach me at tomk@thomasinterior. com — and I hope you will.

"The only way of finding the limits of the possible is by going beyond them into the impossible."

— **ARTHUR C. CLARKE** (1917–2008), British science fiction author and inventor

APPENDICES:
TOOLKIT FOR A WORKPLACE REVOLUTION

In this part of the book, I point you toward what I think are the best resources available on the Web for the person taking the lead role in any campaign to transform a workplace environment and make it a truly great place to work. Each of the following capsule reviews is assigned to one of the following three categories:

APPENDIX A: "HOW TO START THE REVOLUTION" WEBSITES: Visit these websites first; they'll give you a solid grounding in all the good work that's now being done around the country and throughout the world in the areas of workplace design, productivity, and employee motivation and retention.

APPENDIX B: INDUSTRY AND EMPLOYEE-SPECIFIC

WEBSITES: These give you insights into the very best places to work in specific industries or fields of employment. Some offer insights on the best employers targeting a certain demographic group. Most give you access to best practices employed by the companies on the list. These websites are worth looking at closely, even if you don't happen to work in the field in question, because many of the best practices transfer over into other industries and occupations.

APPENDIX C: RESOURCE WEBSITES: These offer tools you can use and also some insights on avoiding some of the most common mistakes made by organizations who undertake a workplace transformation initiative.

APPENDIX A:
"HOW TO START THE REVOLUTION" WEBSITES

1. Herman Miller and Brand Advocacy

http://www.greatplacetowork.com/publications-and-events/ publications/222-article-herman-miller-a-brand-advocacy

Here is where you want to start. The commitment of the office furniture leader Herman Miller to supporting a long-term Great

Workplace Revolution is absolute, and the company is my single favorite role model for each of the strategies outlined in this book. In addition to taking a look at this article and learning about the company's deeply ingrained culture of putting employees first, I strongly suggest that you read Max DePree's fine book *Leadership Is An Art* for more on this global leader in workplace engagement. The more you learn about this company, the more viable best practices you will find to model. In particular, I should note that Herman Miller's strong research and development commitment to the workplace environment is unparalleled.

In Their Own Words

"The making of a company's brand is not just the responsibility of the marketing department; it's in the hands of all of its employees. Spurred by movements such as social media, workers are ever more capable of building up their employer's reputation or tearing it down."

How does a leader inspire brand advocacy in employees? Brian Walker, CEO of Herman Miller, shared his perspective at the 2011 Great Place to Work® Conference in Denver, Colorado.

Waging The Workplace Revolution

"It seems obvious that it's not a question of what role employees play. They are the only ones who build your corporate reputation." — Brian Walker, CEO, Herman Miller

Who Should Visit The Website?

Anyone and everyone interested in launching an ergonomically sound workplace transformation that builds trust, cohesion, and performance.

2. Great Place to Work Institute

http://www.greatplacetowork.com/home

Home page for the premier national organization for promoting values that improve working environments, increase employee retention, and deliver an improved workplace experience. Dedicated to helping companies improve corporate performance and raise the quality of work life for their employees.

In Their Own Words

"Great Place to Work Institute is a global research, consulting and training firm that helps organizations identify, create, and sustain great workplaces through the development of high-trust workplace cultures. We serve businesses, non-profits, and government agencies in 45 countries on all six continents. Our clients are those companies and organizations that wish to maintain Best Company environments, those that are ready to dramatically improve the culture within their workplaces, and those in between the two. We know that organizations that build trust and create a rewarding cycle of personal contribution and appreciation create workplace cultures that deliver outstanding business performance.

"Great Place to Work® began with an unexpected discovery. In 1981 a New York editor asked two business journalists—Robert Levering and Milton Moskowitz—to write a book called *The 100 Best Companies to Work for in America.* Though the pair were skeptical they could find 100 companies that would qualify, they agreed, starting a journey that would lead to more than 25 years of researching, recognizing, and building great workplaces. What was the core insight uncovered by the pair's extensive research? It was that the key to creating a great workplace was not a prescriptive set of employee benefits, programs, and practices, but the building of high-quality relationships in the workplace—relationships characterized by trust, pride, and camaraderie.

"These relationships weren't a 'soft' activity, but key drivers that help improve an organization's business performance. The role of trust in the workplace became core not only for that first, pioneering 1984 book, but its 1988 sequel, *A Great Place to Work: What Makes Some Employers So Good—And Most So Bad.*"

Waging the Workplace Revolution

"We start with a profound respect for organizations considered by their employees to be great workplaces. The leaders of these companies are our heroes, and we stand in awe of what those organizations represent—beacons of hope in what is too often a sea of workplace mediocrity. We believe change can best be achieved by encouraging organizations to aspire to become their best rather than demanding that they fix what is wrong. That's why our approach is positive. By focusing on the examples set by great workplaces, we spread the good news that any company anywhere can follow in their footsteps. From studying the world's best workplaces, we have learned that trust is the key differentiator. This applies to all organizations regardless of national culture, industry, size, or age. By raising the level of trust in the workplace, companies everywhere can improve their business results since cooperation and innovation depend on trust... We believe in changing the quality of work life for all employees throughout the world. As pioneers of this social movement, we encourage all those who wish to create their own great workplaces. Like us, they wish to build a better society for all employees everywhere."

Who Should Visit the Website?

Anyone and everyone interested in launching a workplace transformation that builds trust, cohesion, and performance in the long term. Remarkably wide range of articles, resources, and archive materials.

3. The Gallup Great Workplace Award

http://www.gallup.com/consulting/25312/gallup-great-workplace-award.aspx

Annual award celebrating innovations in the workplace sponsored by the prominent polling and consulting organization founded by George Gallup.

In Their Own Words

"The world's top-performing companies help lead the global economy by engaging their workforces. These companies understand that employee engagement is a force that drives real business outcomes. The Gallup Great Workplace Award was created to recognize these excellent companies for their extraordinary ability to create an engaged workplace culture. Organizations can apply each year for this award.

"Gallup has studied human nature and behavior for more than 75 years. Gallup's reputation for delivering relevant, timely, and visionary research on what people around the world think and feel is the cornerstone of the organization. Gallup employs many of the world's leading scientists in management, economics, psychology, and sociology, and our consultants assist leaders in identifying and monitoring behavioral economic indicators worldwide. Gallup consultants help organizations boost organic growth by increasing customer engagement and maximizing employee productivity through measurement tools, coursework, and strategic advisory services. Gallup's 2,000 professionals deliver services at client organizations, through the Web, at Gallup University's campuses, and in more than 40 offices around the world."

Waging the Workplace Revolution

"Whether you manage a few people, lead a large group, or run an entire organization, you are already in the business of managing employee wellbeing. Every day, in most organizations, there are employees who don't show up, don't give their best effort, erode organizational productivity, and cost their employers millions of dollars because of poor mental and physical health. Conversely, there are employees who engage their colleagues and customers, generate new ideas, and save their employers thousands of dollars in healthcare costs. The wellbeing of your workers has a direct impact, for better or worse, on your organization's bottom line.

"'Worldwide, there are more than two actively disengaged employees for every engaged employee. The organizations we are honoring are ones that have worked hard to shatter and reverse what is typical and they average nine engaged employees for every actively disengaged employee,' notes Jim Harter, Ph.D., Gallup's Chief Scientist of workplace management and wellbeing and coauthor of *Wellbeing: The Five Essential Elements.*"

Who Should Visit the Website

Employers in search of best practices in the area of employee engagement; researchers and social scientists studying workplace engagement.

4. Glassdoor.com's 50 Best Places to Work

Employees rank their workplaces anonymously, and share just how much confidence they have in the senior leader of the organization. An excellent resource for first-hand information about what the "cream of the crop" is doing right ... but make sure to move on to the main Glassdoor.com site, too.

http://www.glassdoor.com/Best-Places-to-Work-LST_KQ0,19.htm

In Their Own Words

"Glassdoor is a free career community where anyone can find and anonymously share an inside look at jobs and companies. What sets us apart is that all our information comes from current and former employees, interview candidates, and even the companies themselves. Now with more than a million salaries, company reviews, interview questions, office photos, and more, you have all the information you'll need to manage your career and make more informed career decisions.

Plus, with Glassdoor's proprietary JobScope™ technology job seekers have a new way to browse job listings and get instant, in-depth details about thousands of companies, including reviews from employees, salary information, recent news coverage, and more.

No other career or jobs site offers such detailed information about specific jobs at specific companies—all for free.

"The Glassdoor Best Places to Work list represents Employees' Choice, identifying the top 50 workplaces, according to employees who have completed surveys on Glassdoor. The ranking is determined by overall rating on Glassdoor, which is determined using a 20-question company survey that captures employees' attitudes about: Career Opportunities, Communication, Compensation & Benefits, Employee Morale, Recognition & Feedback, Senior Leadership, Work/Life Balance, and Fairness & Respect."

Waging The Workplace Revolution

(From a Fluor entry, posted by a recent intern:)

"Pros: Very good people to work with, at least at this site. Very good manager. Nice and easy to work with. Sensible and reasonable. Pays well for an internship. Includes per diem. Nobody running around trying to slit each other's throats. Cons: Far away from home for me. May not get the salary I want if I get hired when I graduate. Other than that, really no down side."

Who Should Visit The Website?

Employees looking for information on specific employers; employers looking for sources of non-industry-specific best practices. Note: The full Glassdoor.com site may have information on other employers in your industry... and could even have anonymous employee reviews of your company!

5. Glassdoor.com's 25 Companies for Work-Life Balance

An interesting, employees-speak variation on the Glassdoor site's popular list of 50 top employers. The beauty of the various Glassdoor.com category rankings is that they are drawn entirely from anonymous on-line employee assessments. This list, which ranks employers in terms of the value I would categorize as understanding and accommodating the whole employee, is one where employers are likely to believe they are doing a better job than they actually are. The ranking of the top 25 companies thus serves as a window into best practices and also as a necessary wakeup call for those executives brave enough to do a search on their own company name to find out how their enterprise stacks up against the best in class!

http://www.glassdoor.com/Top-Companies-for-Work-Life-Balance-LST_KQ0,35.htm

In Their Own Words

"Employees have reported how their companies rate for balancing work with personal life. Find out which 25 companies provide the best work-life balance!"

Waging The Workplace Revolution

"[Purina PetCare is a place] where can you bring not only your passion, your uniqueness, your creativity... but you can bring your dogs and cats too! Sounds like chaos, but it isn't even close. It is a rewarding, kind environment (who can say that about their workplace?), where learning and development are more than encouraged, it is embraced by the leadership. It is such a great environment to work in and the people who work there are amazing people. But it isn't all just fun and learning. The employees work super hard (mostly because they want to) and play just as hard. They care about the products we make and are committed to our brands and what we do for our customers. There is a lot of pride in what we do and that makes it a great environment. I love my job at Nestlé Purina; but most of all, I know most of us feel the same and respond annually to an internal survey to say just that (what company even gets response rates about 90% on employee surveys like we do?). We get it, because the employees know their feedback is important and we continue to strive to work together to always make it better. I cannot imagine working elsewhere." — from an anonymous on-line Glassdoor.com review ranking Purina Petcare as a five out of five employer for work-life balance

6. *Working Mother Magazine's Best Companies for Work/ Life Balance*

http://www.workingmother.com/best-companies

A similar list, but one targeting companies sensitive to the requirements of working mothers. The list offers loads of role models and best practices. Here you will find the cream of the crop of US companies that have made a clear commitment to attracting and retaining the most talented and creative moms.

In Their Own Words

"Twenty-five years ago, *Working Mother* made a bold decision to launch our first Best Companies initiative. The magazine was six years old, covering the immense influx of women into the workforce at the exact moment that American businesses were trying to reinvent themselves to survive yet more economic turmoil. That's when we challenged companies to address the unique needs of working mothers. Today, we celebrate our winners' continued commitment to their employees through an ever-increasing array of family-friendly benefits. The new class of *Working Mother* 100 Best Companies sets the bar higher than ever before, each one offering a menu of benefits including formal and informal flexibility—with flextime, telecommuting, and temporary part-time work options, to name only a few. Showing just how well these companies continue to respond to the needs of working mothers at all stages of their lives, all winners also provide private lactation rooms as well as help finding elder-care services."

Waging the Workplace Revolution

"Abbott: Mothers who work at this health-care company don't need to skip their kids' choir practices or school plays just to impress the boss: Last year, 89% of employees held jobs that permitted them to flex their schedules, while 64% were able to telecommute. Such arrangements suit moms like Diane Weishaar, a program manager for Global Pharmaceutical Operations: 'Having flexible work options has allowed me to spend valuable time with my family and develop a productive, growing career,' says Diane, who has two sons. An on-site child-care center at headquarters looks after kids full-time and can offer therapy for those with special needs; employees elsewhere access tuition discounts at local centers. Parents at the Bioresearch Center in Worcester, MA, or at various California locations of the medical optics and vascular divisions get up to $35 per day for backup care, five days per year."

Who Should Visit the Website?

Mothers in search of better opportunities; employers looking for insights on supporting the whole employee, specifically female employees with kids.

7. 101 Best and Brightest Competition

An annual competition identifying US employers who stand out as having made the lives of their employees better, and also as having given something back to the community. Companies are evaluated in a variety of categories, and the winners, selected within size categories, are profiled on the website. Participants have the option of reviewing detailed confidential assessments on their performance in a number of areas, including compensation and benefits, employee education and development, recruitment, recognition and retention, communication, and diversity. The competition is currently conducted in four geographical areas: Atlanta, Chicago, Metro Detroit, and western Michigan, with plans to expand across the US.

http://www.101bestandbrightest.com/

In Their Own Words

"Designed to aid employers in evaluating strengths and weaknesses of their company, HR function, and employee engagement levels, and also assist in identification and elimination of potential areas of concern."

Waging the Workplace Revolution

"A visit to Armchair will reveal one of our core strengths: In a weaving together of business and creative, everyone takes ownership of the work. Project managers, technologists, and strategists attend brainstorm meetings; designers and writers are involved in client relations. We are inventors and advisers, with talents and personalities across the spectrum." — from a profile of 2011 winner Armchair Media (www.armchairmedia.com).

Who Should Visit the Website?

Managers, senior executives, and the Great Workplace Revolution Coach; job seekers in Atlanta, Chicago, Metro Detroit, and western Michigan.

APPENDIX B: TOP INDUSTRY AND EMPLOYEE-SPECIFIC WEBSITES

1. COMPUTERWORLD'S BEST PLACES TO WORK IN INFORMATION TECHNOLOGY

In Their Own Words

An annually updated survey of the most dynamic and employee-focused enterprises in the IT sector.

http://www.computerworld.com/s/article/9216935/Best_Places_to_Work_in_IT_2011

In Their Own Words

"Each contact at more than 500 nominated companies received a 75-question survey asking about the organizations' average salary and bonus increases, percentage of IT staffers promoted, IT staff turnover rates, training and development, and the percentage of women and minorities in IT staff and management positions... Participants were asked to provide the name and contact information of an appropriate individual at their company who was familiar with or had access to employment statistics, financial data, and information about benefits policies and programs for the IT department and the company as a whole."

Waging The Workplace Revolution

"My No. 1 favorite thing about working at USAA is being on a team that has a single goal," says Emily Bubela, a senior research engineer and self-described military brat, who joined the company eight years ago, right out of college. Growing up in a military family, the first check Bubela ever wrote was on a USAA account, and she has had car insurance with the company since she was a teenager.

"USAA has been in my DNA for a long time," she quips. Now, working at the company, "there's never a question about everybody's priorities. It's always the same. What's best for the member is the guiding principle," she says.

"We have a strong and noble mission, and we believe in it," says Jackie Head, executive director of database and storage management. Every month, one of the company's military members is profiled in a short video. "It gives us a sense of the people we serve," Head says. "It's that emotional side that keeps you very much in sync with who your customers are." (For more information on this company, visit www.usaa.com.)

Who Should Visit the Website?

Prospective job seekers and employers within the IT sector seeking to learn about best practices. The articles on individual companies are detailed and well written.

2. Advertising Age's Best Places to Work

An annually updated list of top employers in the advertising industry celebrating employers in the marketing, media, and advertising industry that have created environments where employees "love to work and contribute their best ideas." A joint effort of *Advertising Age* and Best Companies Group, a firm that conducts "best places to work" programs across the country.

http://adage.com/article/news/advertising-age-s-places-work-2011/148782/

In Their Own Words

"Despite or even in light of economic challenges, there are companies that are thriving in their commitments to their employees and to their work. They are workplaces that cultivate camaraderie, reward creativity, and spur innovation. They're winning accounts, customers, and talent eager to contribute to organizations they believe in. And those are the Best Places to Work in Marketing & Media.

"Any agency, media owner, or marketer with more than 50 full-time employees is eligible. The Best Places to Work will be determined by the results of two surveys. Your company will complete the first survey detailing hiring practices, benefits, and pay. Employees also will have a say through a second employee-driven survey. The surveys will be conducted by our research partner, Buck Consultants LLC. The combined score of the company and employee surveys will determine the Best Places to Work."

Waging the Workplace Revolution

"BGT Partners may not be the first job for its employees, but for many it is the last. The Miami-headquartered interactive marketing agency has the mantra "Trade your job for a career"—and maintains a nearly 100% retention rate. 'We're usually not the first or even second agency they've worked at,' said David Clarke, co-founder and managing partner at BGT. 'We have a more mature and experienced staff that has seen how other agencies work. It's not about the millions of dollars, it's about customer satisfaction and employee satisfaction.' The agency has a flat management structure and open offices to encourage sharing of experience and knowledge. Any employee with a good idea is encouraged to speak up, and doing so can result in things such as a new job being created, a spot bonus, and/or salary increase for creativity and innovation. (For more information on this company, please visit www.bgtpartners.com.)

"'The entire team wants everyone to succeed,' said Tara McGrath, director-professional services for BGT Chicago. Strategist Adam Nussdorfer agreed, adding, 'BGT encourages you to take your own initiative. If you find something you are passionate about, they'll give you everything you need to pursue it.'"

Who Should Visit the Website?

Employees, employers, and anyone else interested in advertising and marketing.

3. The Scientist's Best Places To Work In Academia

A detailed overview of selected academic workplaces with great, supportive, employee-focused organizational cultures. Includes employers outside the United States. A project of *The Scientist*, magazine of the life sciences.

http://the-scientist.com/2011/07/01/best-places-to-work-academia-2011/

In Their Own Words

"A Web-based survey form was posted at www.the-scientist.com... Results were collected and collated automatically. E-mail invitations were sent to readers of *The Scientist* and registrants on *The Scientist* website who identified themselves as full-time life scientists working in academia or noncommercial research institutions. The survey was also publicized on *The Scientist* website and through news stories. 2,260 useable and qualified responses were received... Employees were asked an in-depth set of questions that result in an analysis in 8 core areas: leadership and planning; culture and communications; role satisfaction; working environment; relationship with supervisor; training and development; pay and benefits; overall satisfaction.

"In addition, we ranked institutions based on unweighted average scores for the 9 major topic categories covered by the statements included in the survey. These categories are: job satisfaction; peers; infrastructure and environment; research resources; pay; management and policies; teaching and mentoring; tenure and promotion."

Waging the Workplace Revolution

"Set in the idyllic town of Dundee on the eastern coast of Scotland, the College of Life Sciences at the University of Dundee boasts a world-class life sciences research community. With no doors or walls to keep them separate, its nearly 500 full-time researchers toil away in open laboratories within eyesight of each other. 'We're a high-powered research environment in a low-pressure living environment,' says Dean of Research Mike Ferguson... In the past decade, the university has spun out more than 20 companies that have generated some 500 jobs in the city of Dundee alone, earning the respect of the local community."

Who Should Visit the Website?

Research-focused employers and employees.

4. The Scientist's Best Places to Work in Industry

*http://classic.the-scientist.com/fragments/bptw/2011/
industry/bptw_industry_top40_2011.jsp*

A companion list to the magazine's popular list of academic employ-ers. This summary focuses on the private sector.

In Their Own Words

"By forging new relationships and finding novel uses for existing technologies, the companies topping this year's survey are employing creative ways to advance science and expand their markets."

Waging the Workplace Revolution

"Epizyme, an epigenetics research company based in Cambridge, MA, placed 1st overall and among small companies. Their discoveries have spawned deals with large pharmaceutical companies to further epigenetics drug development and therapeutics. Epizyme's newfound collaborations are a big change for the small company, and the employees are excited about what's to come. 'It feels like an endorsement of the quality of the science we're doing,' says Christina

Allain, who develops cell-based assays for the company. 'It's a great morale boost..."

Who Should Visit the Website?

Research-focused employers and employees.

5. Inc. Magazine's Top Small Company Workplaces

The annual list of exemplary small employers is a joint project of *Inc.* magazine and Winning Workplaces, a nonprofit organization based in Evanston, Illinois.

http://www.inc.com/top-workplaces/index.html

In Their Own Words

"Qualifying companies must be based in North America and privately held, and must have been in operation at least three years at the end of 2010. They can have no more than 500 full-time employees. Not-for-profit organizations are eligible. This year, roughly 350 companies applied, and Winning Workplaces's staff and a panel of independent judges whittled that down to 50 winners. Applicants were judged on employee engagement and development, management effectiveness, rewards and recognition, mission, and benefits. In addition, Winning Workplaces conducted anonymous employee-satisfaction surveys at all finalist companies...

"Some entrepreneurs possess clear visions of their ideal cultures from the beginning. Every decision they make—whom to hire, what benefits to provide, where the CEO should sit—is in pursuit of those ideals. In fact, the opportunity to derive an entire social order from the leader's character and experience can be an incentive for starting a company in the first place. So is the urge to do things differently from those unenlightened bosses who made the entrepreneur's life hell back when he was working for the Man. Ask a founder why he designed his company a certain way, and he's as likely to tell you what he was reacting against as what he was striving for... The leaders of these companies don't view jobs as prizes doled out to lucky applicants. Rather, they figure the people they have chosen have chosen them as well, and, naturally, they want to make the place nice for them. So they treat workers fairly, often generously; respect their personal lives; provide opportunities for development; and endow their jobs with meaning and fun. In return, those employees bestow their best ideas and efforts on the business. They pull together through change and hard times."

Waging the Workplace Revolution

"At Emma, what's most important is an open, collaborative environment where transparency is key. Emma's CEO, Clint Smith, says this philosophy goes beyond an open floor plan and weekly meetings. It's about creating an 'energy,' he says, that makes employees feel like they're not just doing work—that they're having fun too. 'We like to blend social and work,' Smith says. Each year, the company hosts an open mic talent show open to Emma employees at a local bar in Nashville. 'We take work very seriously, but we have a whole lot of fun getting there,' Smith says."

Who Should Visit the Website?

Prospective employees interested in finding jobs at smaller, dynamic companies; company founders and senior executives interested in organizational best practices of these companies.

6. Nyreport.com's 10 Great Entrepreneurial Employers

How do small, innovative startup businesses compete for top talent—and retain that talent? The companies on this list offer some answers. Note: *New York Report* is the only media company exclusively serving NY tri-state area small/midsize business market. Ten times a year, it produces a magazine full of helpful resources, advice, news, and stories for area business owners.

http://www.nyreport.com/great_places_to_work_2011

In Their Own Words

"What makes a business a great place to work and what makes it a great entrepreneurial place to work are vastly different qualities. Offering robust benefits and high salaries is great, but creating an environment that encourages teamwork and creativity is usually more important for growing businesses. For talented employees all over the region, the ability to help build something and watch their efforts directly contribute to the success of a company is an enticing offer. Personal growth, freedom of expression, recognition of talent, and having ownership over what they do every day carries a high value for many workers and proves to help smaller, independent companies compete for talent with the big businesses offering big compensation."

Waging the Workplace Revolution

"Before founding DiGennaro Communications (DGC), Samantha DiGennaro had a lot of experience working at big PR agencies. While she may have loved what she was doing, she says the companies felt 'soulless.' To create a warm and exciting environment, the loft-style offices of DGC have a ping-pong table, a Nintendo Wii, and wine night on Fridays. The company also has a social committee that plans team activities like bowling and trips to the Shake Shack in Madison Square Park. DGC is emphatic about celebrating success. One method of recognizing achievements made by the staff is 'The Hit Board,' a spot in the office where team members can post their greatest accomplishments for the month. On the last day of each month, all the employees gather around the wall, vote on the top 'hit' and award prizes to the top three. Prizes have included $30 dollar gift card to Best Buy for top prize $10 Starbucks for runners up. The team then awards a 'hit of the year' at year's end."

Who Should Visit the Website?

Employees in search of employment and internship leads in entrepreneurial work environments in and around New York City; entrepreneurs in search of best practices for attracting and retaining the most creative people.

7. 20 Best Places To Work For Recent Grads

An annual summary of great workplaces for college graduates entering the job market. A joint project of the Experience.com and the Salary.com websites.

http://www.experience.com/entry-level-jobs/
2011-best-places-to-work/

In Their Own Words

"While college seniors are excited about closing the door on one part of their life, it's common for them to feel pressure as it pertains to next steps. Some graduates may have already landed a job, but others may still not have a clue as to how to start their job search or what type of company they want to work for. So where are the best places to work for those just graduating? Experience.com has done the research and compiled a list of the top 20 Best Places to Work for Recent Grads. The companies on this list range from a wide variety of industries, and they're hiring! In fact, these companies plan to hire nearly 20,000 recent graduates in the next year alone. This list is designed to showcase companies around the country with great entry-level hiring practices, and to educate recent grads on what to look for in a company."

Waging the Workplace Revolution

"Recent grads who are up for an intellectual challenge will certainly find it at ZS Associates. This company makes it to the top 20 list again simply because they are committed to taking entry-level hires to the next level. Recent grads will be given a wide range of projects and get to rapidly develop their expertise. This helps new hires thrive within the company and prepares them for future roles. Within

6 months, associates may help redesign the structure of a 3000+-person sales force or help design and administer a sales incentive plan. In this work-hard atmosphere, colleagues are friends, an ethos of cooperation predominates, and innovation is demanded from employees and clients. Expected Number of Recent College Grads to Hire in 2011: Full-Time – 325; Intern – 100."

Who Should Visit the Website?

Recent college grads in search of employment and internship leads; employers in search of best practices targeting this group.

8. Best Employers for Employees Over 50

The annual list is compiled and sponsored by the American Association of Retired Persons, better known as AARP. AARP is a nonprofit, nonpartisan membership organization for people age 50 and over, whose mission is to enhance the quality of life for all of us as we age.

http://www.aarp.org/work/employee-benefits/best_employers/

In Their Own Words

"The aging of the workforce in today's global economy presents not only challenges, but also opportunities and advantages for employers willing to innovate and adapt. The AARP Best Employers for Workers

Over 50 program awards businesses and organizations that have implemented new and innovative policies and best practices in talent management. These organizations are creating roadmaps for others on how to attract and retain top talent in today's multigenerational workforce...

"Areas of consideration (for inclusion on the annual list) include: recruiting practices; opportunities for training, education, and career development; workplace accommodations; alternative work options, such as flexible scheduling, job-sharing, and phased retirement; employee health and pension benefits; benefits for retirees."

Waging the Workplace Revolution

"Job advancement at Cornell University is formalized in the university's Qualified Employees Seeking Transfer, or 'QUEST' program, which is a performance-based arrangement designed to help employees identify opportunities for internal transfers. Retirees benefit from continued access to life insurance, the employee assistance plan, the wellness program, and long-term-care insurance at rates that are the same or similar to those paid by active employees. The Cornell Retiree Association provides for emeritus employees' continued engagement with the university through library and fitness-center privileges, continuing education, access to the computer lab, and volunteer opportunities."

Who Should Visit the Website?

Prospective employees over the age of 50; senior executives interested in attracting and retaining the most experienced, talented, and creative older workers.

9. Best Places to Work in the Federal Government

The Federal government is America's largest employer. It is made up of thousands of smaller employers —agencies, subagencies, departments, bureaus, oversight boards, and countless other organizations— with divergent workplace philosophies and workplace cultures. This website spotlights those parts of the government that generate the best employee satisfaction scores.

http://bestplacestowork.org/BPTW/rankings/

In Their Own Words

"The Best Places to Work rankings—the most comprehensive and authoritative rating of employee satisfaction and commitment in the federal government—are produced by the Partnership for Public Service. The Best Places to Work rankings are the most comprehensive and authoritative rating and analysis of employee satisfaction and commitment in the federal government."

Waging the Workplace Revolution

(The Nuclear Regulatory Commission) has Best Places Index scores that exceed government-wide norms, as well as greater-than-normal alignment between staff and managers on key workforce issues. These results suggest that an agency is well positioned to maintain and improve on current efforts and to recognize shared challenges in order to better address them."

Who Should Visit the Website?

Prospective and current federal managers and employees.

10. Industry Week's 50 Best Places to Work in Manufacturing

A national survey and recognition program managed by Best Companies Group and sponsored by *Industry Week* magazine.

http://bestplacestoworkmanufacturing.com/

In Their Own Words

"Dedicated to identifying and recognizing the best employers in the manufacturing industry."

Waging the Workplace Revolution

"As a manufacturing leader, you know how incredibly important your workplace culture is to the success of your enterprise. Build a team of committed individuals focused on a common purpose and you've gone a long way to unlocking the energy and ideas needed for success. So it is more critical than ever that companies have unbiased, reliable insight into what their employees think about company leadership, communications, work environment, training, supervision, and other key issues."

Who Should Visit the Website?

Manufacturing- and heavy-industry-focused employers and employees.

II. Best Nonprofts to Work For

A survey and recognition program dedicated to finding and recognizing the best US employers in the nonprofit sector. Managed by the Best Companies Group and sponsored by the *NonProfit Times*.

http://bestnonprofitstoworkfor.com/

In Their Own Words

"Best Companies Group will survey up to 400 randomly selected employees in a nonprofit depending on workforce size. We encourage all nonprofits to use our free online survey process. However, if online surveys will not work for your nonprofit, we offer a traditional paper-based survey option. All employee information is submitted anonymously."

Waging the Workplace Revolution

"Established in 1980, The Rideshare Company is committed to improving the daily business commute for those who live and work in the Northeastern United States with innovative transportation solutions, Rideshare is able to meet its goal day after day, which is to make trips to work easier, less costly, more convenient, and environmentally friendly." — Concise mission statement of The Rideshare Company, one of the 2010 winners.

Who Should Visit the Website?

Executives and employees of nonprofit organizations; jobseekers in search of employment opportunities within the best work environments in the nonprofit sector.

12. Best Accounting Firms to Work For

A survey and recognition program dedicated to finding and recognizing the best US employers in the field of accounting. Managed by the Best Companies Group and sponsored by *Accounting Today* and ADP.

http://bestaccountingfirmstoworkfor.com/

In Their Own Words

"To be considered for participation, companies had to be a publicly or privately held US accounting firm with at least 15 employees. Firms from across the country entered the two-part selection process... The first part consisted of evaluating each nominated firm's practices, philosophy, systems, and demographics. The second part consisted of an employee survey to measure the employee experience."

Waging the Workplace Revolution

"Johnson Jacobson Wilcox (JJW) believes that giving back is the only way for a community to move forward. As an organization, we foster an attitude of contribution and support of others. As individuals, we choose JJW because of that attitude and the support we feel from each other. Join us in supporting the community of Las Vegas by giving back." — Statement of a core workplace value from Nevada-based Johnson Jacobson Wilcox, one of the 2010 winners in the 15-49 employees category.

Who Should Visit the Website?

Executives and employees of accounting firms; jobseekers in search of employment opportunities within the best work environments in the accounting sector.

13. Best Places to Work in Collections

A survey and recognition program dedicated to finding and

recognizing the best US employers in the field of collections. Managed by the Best Companies Group and sponsored by InsideArm.com.

http://bestplacestoworkcollections.com/

In Their Own Words

"(We conduct) a simple yet thorough company assessment. The assessment is a two-part process designed to gather detailed data about each participating collections company. In part one, the employer completes a questionnaire and in part two, employees of the company complete an employee survey... [This produces] a detailed set of data enabling the analysts to determine the strengths and opportunities of the participating companies. The workplaces are ranked based on this data and then the Employer Benchmark Summary is returned to each participating company."

Waging the Workplace Revolution

"We love Best Places to Work because not only does it provide us valuable anonymous feedback from our team, it allows us to see where we rank among other collection agencies. Let's face it—ours is not the easiest industry to recruit for, nor is it a popular job, so knowing we are doing all we can to make and keep American Profit Recovery a great place to work is key to our ownership and management team. I feel great pride each year when we hang our Best Places to Work award in our conference room. We get many comments from interviews and vendors who visit our offices, and many congratulations from our clients when they hear the news. We have participated and been ranked for three years now, and used the feedback we've received each year to make APR a little bit better of a place to work. We appreciate this program, the feedback it provides, and the acknowledgment of being one of the best." — Michelle Riviello, American Profit Recovery

Who Should Visit the Website?

Executives and employees of collections firms; jobseekers in search of employment opportunities within the best work environments in the collections industry.

APPENDIX C: TOP RESOURCE WEBSITES

I. KOLBE CORP.

Don't call it personality testing! Thought leader Kathy Kolbe is both a pioneer and a cutting-edge innovator in the field of *conative* research. If you don't know what that word means, then you definitely need to hear what she has to say about how you and your team can work together better. The Kolbe Index identifies each individual's **critical initial instincts relative to work and learning activities.** These instincts are also known by names like "modus operandi" or "natural strengths." Before Kathy's work, they were poorly understood. Understanding how our own conative instincts operate, and how those of others do, is an overlooked but essential first step for managers and, for that matter, anyone else in the organization.

When teams are not in harmony, the cause is usually some kind of conative mismatch!

http://Kolbe.com

In Their Own Words

"Synergy doesn't just happen by chance. It takes the right mix of instinctive talents in the right roles. Kolbe identifies this formula for success with an extraordinary level of accuracy and detail. Kolbe's Leadership Analytics™ solutions don't just identify the cause of team productivity problems. They deliver strategies to solve them. By relating the instinctive strengths of team members to the factors that determine group success, Leadership Analytics™ provides managers and leaders with proof-of-improvement metrics for a wide range of group challenges.

"A complete set of Leadership Analytics™ documents contains up to seventy-five pages chock full of insights and bottom-line findings to help team leaders pinpoint sources of conflict, break through group inertia and organizational paralysis, accommodate differing approaches to problem solving, align team member expectations with supervisor requirements, inventory the collection of instinctive strengths on the team, accomplish more with fewer people, and improve individual and group productivity.

No other organizational development software can match the breadth and detailed analysis of Leadership Analytics. For more information e-mail us or call (800) 642-2822.

Waging The Workplace Revolution

"Kathy Kolbe was the first to identify four universal human instincts used in creative problem-solving. These instincts are not measurable. However, the observable acts derived from them can be identified and quantified by the Kolbe A™ Index. These instinct-driven behaviors are represented in the four Kolbe Action Modes:

- Fact Finder—the instinctive way we gather and share information.

- Follow Through—the instinctive way we arrange and design.

- Quick Start—the instinctive way we deal with risk and uncertainty.

- Implementor—the instinctive way we handle space and tangibles.

Who Should Visit The Website?

Any human being who has to work, at some point during the day, with another human being.

2. Glassdoor.Com

Welcome to the revolution; it began while you weren't looking! If your employees have not yet started posting anonymous reviews on this site explaining exactly what it is really like to work at your organization, rest assured that they soon will. Yes, you have to put the reviews in context... but in order to do that, you must first read the reviews and learn all you possibly can from them!

http://www.glassdoor.com

In Their Own Words

"Glassdoor is your free inside look at jobs and companies. Salary details, company reviews, and interview questions—all posted anonymously by employees and job seekers."

Waging the Workplace Revolution

"Tell your company's story with an Enhanced Employer Profile. Highlight your employment brand, promote your latest job listings, and get access to advanced analytics and competitive benchmarking."

Who Should Visit the Website?

Managers, senior executives, and the Great Workplace Revolution Coach. You may choose not to encourage employees to visit the site, given the ample number of possible job search leads they will find there. At the same time, however, you should not be at all surprised when they decide to visit the site on their own. Monitor references to your company on this site now... so you can fix problems and avoid defections!

3. Only One Workplace Plan?

Must-read debunking of the common, flawed tactic of building workplace culture initiatives around specific strategic goals. Offers insights on how senior executives can put together a better, more flexible plan.

http://www.computerworld.com/s/article/357132/Only_One_Workforce_Plan_It_s_Time_to_Think_Ahead

In Their Own Words

"Most organizations identify goals for the coming year and then structure their workforce plans to help achieve those goals. This method, however, doesn't take into account the many factors that can affect or alter organizational goals and ultimately require course corrections to workforce plans."

Waging the Workplace Revolution

"Multiple projected workforce plans are needed to address the most likely scenarios a company could face as it moves toward its strategic objectives. To do this, managers must make communication a high priority and ultimately improve their leadership abilities. Managers must understand the intended strategic direction of their organizations and how it translates into a functional plan for their teams. They must also make sure that the probable scenarios that could change the strategic plan are understood by all parties. Communicating all this to the team creates an opportunity for engagement that is incredibly valuable."

Who Should Visit the Website?

Managers, senior executives, and the Great Workplace Revolution Coach.

***

BIBLIOGRAPHY

4imprint.com (2009). *The Benefits and Methods of Continuing Employee Education*, published by 4imprint.com

Amabile, Teresa (2011). *The Progress Principle: Using Small Wins to Ignite Joy, Engagement, and Creativity at Work*, Harvard Business Press.

Anderson, Lydia E. and Bolt, Sandra B. (2010). *Professionalism: Skills for Workplace Success (2nd Edition)*, Prentice-Hall.

Bates, Suzanne (2011). *Discover Your CEO Brand: Secrets to Embracing and Maximizing Your Unique Value as a Leader*, McGraw-Hill.

Beckstrom, Rod A. and Brafman, Ori (2008). *The Starfish and the Spider: The Unstoppable Power of Leaderless Organizations*, Portfolio Trade.

Berkun, Scott (2010). *The Myths of Innovation*, O'Reilly Media.

Branham, Leigh and Hirschfeld, Mark (2010). *Re-Engage: How America's Best Places to Work Inspire Extra Effort in Extraordinary Times*, McGraw-Hill.

Burchell, Michael and Robin, Jennifer (2011). *The Great Workplace: How to Build It, How to Keep It, and Why It Matters*, Jossey-Bass.

Cameron, Kim S. and Quinn, Robert E. (2011). *Diagnosing and Chang-*

ing Organizational Culture: Based on the Competing Values Framework, Jossey-Bass.

Chester, Eric (2012). *Reviving Work Ethic: A Leader's Guide to Ending Entitlement and Restoring Pride in the Emerging Workforce*, Greenleaf Book Group Press.

Conaty, Bill and Charan, Ram (2010). *The Talent Masters: Why Smart Leaders Put People Before Numbers*, Crown Business.

Connors, Roger and Smith, Tom (2011). *Change the Culture, Change the Game: The Breakthrough Strategy for Energizing Your Organization and Creating Accountability for Results*, Portfolio Hardcover.

Crowley, Katherine and Elster, Kathi (2007). *Working With You is Killing Me: Freeing Yourself from Emotional Traps at Work*, Business Plus.

Denning, Stephen (2010). *The Leader's Guide to Radical Management: Reinventing the Workplace for the 21st Century*, Jossey-Bass.

Drucker, Peter F. (1993). *Management: Tasks, Responsibilities, Practices*, Harper Paperbacks.

Ferriss, Timothy (2009). *The 4-Hour Workweek, Expanded and Updated: Expanded and Updated, With Over 100 New Pages of Cutting-Edge Content*, Crown Archetype.

Head, Simon (2005). *The New Ruthless Economy: Work and Power in the Digital Age*, Oxford University Press, USA.

Kanigel, Robert (2005). *The One Best Way: Frederick Winslow Taylor and the Enigma of Efficiency*, The MIT Press.

Levering, Robert (1990). *A Great Place to Work: What Makes Some Employers So Good—And Most So Bad*, Avon Books.

Maxwell, John C. (2006). *The 17 Essential Qualities of a Team Player: Becoming the Kind of Person Every Team Wants*, Thomas Nelson.

Meister, Jeanne C. and Willyerd, Karie (2010). *The 2020 Workplace: How Innovative Companies Attract, Develop, and Keep Tomorrow's Employees Today*, HarperBusiness.

Mintzberg, Henry (2007). *Mintzberg on Management*, Free Press.

Namie, Gary and Namie, Ruth (2009). *The Bully at Work: What You Can Do to Stop the Hurt and Reclaim Your Dignity on the Job*, Sourcebooks.

Pittampalli, Al (2011). *Read This Before Our Next Meeting*, The Domino Project.

Rieger, Tom (2011). *Breaking the Fear Barrier: How Fear Destroys Companies from the Inside Out, and What to Do About It*, Gallup Press.

Sanders, Tim (2006). *The Likeability Factor: How to Boost Your L-Factor and Achieve Your Life's Dreams*, Three Rivers Press.

Simonton, Bennet S. (2005). *Leading People To Be Highly Motivated And Committed*, Simonton Associates.

Sutton, Robert I. (2010). *Good Boss, Bad Boss: How to Be the Best... and Learn from the Worst*, Business Plus.

Taylor, Frederick Winslow (1911). *The Principles of Scientific Management*, Norton Library.

Wagner, Rodd and Harter, James K. (2006). *12: The Elements of Great Managing*, Gallup Press.

Warner, Jim and Klemp, Kaley (2011). *The Drama-Free Office: A Guide to Healthy Collaboration with Your Team, Coworkers, and Boss*, Greenleaf Book Group Press.

Zaffron, Steve and Logan, Dave (2011). *The Three Laws of Performance: Rewriting the Future of Your Organization and Your Life*, Jossey-Bass.

Index

Afterword

No organization is safely successful in today's business environment. The need of leaders to get back to basics is just *so* "last century." Business is moving at warp speed today...and picking up more speed! It's a new game today with new rules and "new basics."

There are four, soon to be five, generations of people (twenty-somethings to seventy-somethings) in the workplace. Each has its own priorities, distinct worldviews, communication preferences, and attitudes toward technology. To benefit from this cross-pollination opportunity, we must learn to interact with, be amazed by, and tailor our workplace environment to meet the needs and strengths of each of these five generations.

This book provides a roadmap to navigate through this most exciting time in recent history. I call it the Synergistic Decade (2010 to 2020). Inside you will find the twelve essential strategies for creating a Great Place To Work to attract and retain the most creative workers of all ages.

Join the Great Workplace Revolution, the revolution where everybody wins.

Tom Klobucher

ABOUT THE AUTHOR

Tom Klobucher is founder and CEO of Thomas Interior Systems, Inc., an office planning and furnishings firm in the Chicago area. As a future-based entrepreneur, Tom has over thirty-five years of experience leading, advising, and mentoring businesses and senior level leaders in the exciting process of creating Great Places To Work. The

Thomas Team has assisted well over 20,000 organizations throughout the Midwest in improving their office work environments to create great places to work.

Tom's new book, *The Great Workplace Revolution*, provides a detailed roadmap for navigating through the next ten years of workplace, demographic, and social change. He believes this period will be the most exciting decade for CEOs, presidents, and company founders in recent history.

Tom's book will prepare you and your enterprise to deal with the vast generational changes already underway in the workplace, and will share the twelve essential strategies for creating a Great Place to Work. In addition, it provides the necessary tools to tailor your workplace to attract, and to retain, the very best people. *The Great Workplace Revolution* will change your way of thinking about bringing true success and fun to the workplace environment.

Tom Klobucher

Thomas Interior Systems

630.980.4200

476 Brighton Dr

Bloomingdale, IL 60108

www.thomasinterior.com

www.thegreatworkplacerevolution.com